The interpretation of the meaning of texts is the central activity of the humanities and social sciences. But are there limits to what a text can be made to mean? Are the author's intentions relevant to establishing these limits? Should some readings be ruled out as 'overinterpretations'?

This book brings together some of the most distinguished figures currently at work in philosophy and in literary theory and criticism. Three new pieces by Umberto Eco, leading semiotic theorist as well as internationally famous novelist, form the core of the book. Here, Eco develops his view of how the 'intention of the work' may set limits to possible interpretations. Then, from their different points of view, the philosopher Richard Rorty, the literary theorist Jonathan Culler, and the critic and novelist Christine Brooke-Rose challenge Eco's argument and elaborate their own distinctive positions. The book concludes with Eco's reply to his critics.

In a substantial introduction, Stefan Collini sets this debate in its historical and institutional context, and explores the ways in which fundamental human values are at stake. This accessible and often entertaining book makes a major contribution to the debate about textual meaning, and will be essential reading for all those interested in literary theory and in the wider issues raised by the question of interpretation.

INTERPRETATION AND OVERINTERPRETATION

Cambridge University Press gratefully acknowledges the co-operation of the President and Fellows
of Clare Hall, Cambridge, under whose auspices
the 1990 Tanner Lectures and Seminar (from which
this book derives) were held.

Interpretation and overinterpretation

UMBERTO ECO

WITH
RICHARD RORTY,
JONATHAN CULLER,
CHRISTINE BROOKE-ROSE

EDITED BY
Stefan Collini

 CAMBRIDGE
UNIVERSITY PRESS

Published by the Press Syndicate of the University of Cambridge
The Pitt Building, Trumpington Street, Cambridge CB2 1RP
40 West 20th Street, New York, NY 10011-4211, USA
10 Stamford Road, Oakleigh, Melbourne 3166, Australia

First published 1992
Reprinted 1992 (three times), 1994

Printed in Great Britain at Athenæum Press, Newcastle upon Tyne

A catalogue record for this book is available from the British Library

Library of Congress cataloguing in publication data
Eco, Umberto.
Interpretation and overinterpretation / Umberto Eco and Richard Rorty,
Jonathan Culler, Christine Brooke-Rose; edited by Stefan Collini.
p.   cm.
ISBN 0-521-40227-1 (hard). – ISBN 0-521-42554-9 (pbk)
1. Criticism.   2. Semiotics and literature.   I. Collini, Stefan, 1947–
PN98.S46E25   1992 801'.95 – dc20
91-4227 CIP

ISBN 0 521 40227 1 hardback
ISBN 0 521 42554 9 paperback

VN

CONTENTS

NOTES ON THE CONTRIBUTORS

UMBERTO ECO is Professor of Semiotics at the University of Bologna.

RICHARD RORTY is University Professor of the Humanities at the University of Virginia.

JONATHAN CULLER is Professor of English and Comparative Literature and Director of the Society for the Humanities, Cornell University.

CHRISTINE BROOKE-ROSE was formerly Professor of Literature at the University of Paris VIII.

STEFAN COLLINI is University Lecturer in English and Fellow of Clare Hall, Cambridge.

Introduction: Interpretation terminable and interminable

STEFAN COLLINI

I

'My only reservation is whether this topic will turn out to be sufficiently about "human values".' Those familiar with the workings of academic committees will recognize the tone. Around the table on this occasion was the Tanner Lectures Committee of Clare Hall, Cambridge. The Tanner Lectures were founded by the American philanthropist and former Professor of Philosophy at the University of Utah, Obert C. Tanner, and they were formally established at Clare Hall on 1 July 1978. (Tanner lectures are also given annually at Harvard, Michigan, Princeton, Stanford, Utah, Brasenose College, Oxford, and occasionally elsewhere.) Their stated purpose is 'to advance and reflect upon the scholarly and scientific learning relating to human values and valuations'. On the occasion in question, an invitation to be the Tanner lecturer for 1990 had been issued to Umberto Eco, and in accepting he had proposed 'Interpretation and overinterpretation' as his topic. It was this topic which led the committee-member quoted above, anxious to anticipate any possible difficulty, to voice his one reservation, a reservation which the committee did not allow to detain it for very long.

It was evidently not a reservation shared by the nearly five hundred people who squeezed into one of Cambridge's largest auditoria to hear the lectures. Perhaps some came largely to satisfy their curiosity by seeing one of the most celebrated writers of our time, perhaps others were driven simply by the desire not to miss a show-piece cultural and social occasion, though the fact that this huge audience returned to hear the second and third lectures testifies to other sources of interest as well as to the magnetic qualities of the lecturer. Still less were any reservations manifested by those enthusiasts who next morning queued from the early hours to be able to listen to, and participate in, the ensuing seminar, spurred in this case by the prospect of seeing Eco debate with Richard Rorty, Jonathan Culler, and Christine Brooke-Rose, in a day-long session chaired by Frank Kermode. Discussion was certainly lively, enriched by contributions from a distinguished gathering of scholars and critics, beginning (alphabetically) with Isobel Armstrong, Gillian Beer, Patrick Boyde, and Marilyn Butler, and seasoned by the specially pertinent reflections of other novelist–critics present, such as Malcolm Bradbury, John Harvey, and David Lodge.

Umberto Eco, the principal participant in these proceedings, has distinguished himself in so many fields that he defies easy classification. A native of Piedmont, he studied philosophy at the University of Turin and wrote a thesis on the aesthetics of St Thomas Aquinas. He worked on cultural programmes for the state television network, and subsequently held posts at the universities of Turin, Milan, and Florence, while continuing to act in an editorial capacity for the publishing house of Bompiani. Since 1975, he has held the Chair of Semiotics at the University of Bologna (the first of its kind to be established in any university). He has published over a dozen substantial books, making important contributions to the fields of aesthetics, semiotics, and cultural criticism. Most of these books have been translated into English and other languages, though it is an indication of Professor Eco's formidable talents as a linguist that several of his recent works have had to be translated into *Italian*, the originals having been written in English. At the same time, he has been a prolific journalist, writing regular and often very funny columns for several of the major Italian daily and weekly newspapers. But, in the English-speaking world at least, he is known to a far wider audience as the author of *The Name of the Rose*, the novel he published in 1980 and which became an international best-seller. In 1988 he followed this with his second novel, *Foucault's Pendulum*, which was translated into English the following year and showered with critical attention.

The present volume includes the revised texts of Eco's 1990 Tanner Lectures, of the papers by the three seminarists, and of Eco's reply. Since the issues disputed among the participants may at times seem rather abstruse or technical to the uninitiated reader, it may be helpful to map out in advance the main lines of division between them and to point to some of the larger implications of an enquiry which lies at the heart of so many forms of cultural understanding in the late twentieth century.

II

Interpretation is not, of course, an activity invented by twentieth-century literary theorists. Indeed, puzzles and disputes about how to characterize that activity have a long history in Western thought, provoked above all by the enormously consequential task of establishing the meaning of the Word of God. The modern phase of this history essentially dates from the heightened self-consciousness about the problem of textual meaning introduced by the biblical hermeneutics associated with Schleiermacher at the beginning of the nineteenth century, and the centrality of interpretation to understanding all the creations of the human spirit was made the basis of a programme for the complete range of the *Geisteswissenschaften* by Dilthey in the later part of the century.

The distinctive stage the debate has entered in the last two or three decades needs to be understood in the context of two large-scale developments. The first is that an enormous expansion of higher education since 1945 throughout the Western world has given a new significance to issues which affect the general cultural role of such institutions and, more particularly, to questions about the identity and status of the institutionally defined 'disciplines'. In the English-speaking world, 'English' as a discipline acquired in the course of this process a position of peculiar centrality and sensitiveness as the discipline the least insulated from the existential concerns of the lay readers and writers outside the walls – which meant, among other things, that disputes within the profession continued to be the object of intermittent public attention. A simple yet striking indication of the subject's prominence is the fact that in 1970 English was the largest undergraduate department in two-thirds of American universities and colleges.[1]

However, in recent decades both the 'canon' of writings traditionally understood to constitute the subject-matter of the discipline and the methods considered appropriate to its study have come under sharper scrutiny, as the social and ethnic

---

[1] Richard Ohmann, *English in America: A Radical View of the Profession* (New York, 1976), pp. 214–15. Ohmann emphasizes the extent to which this expansion rested upon the key curricular role of 'freshman composition'. For a longer historical perspective, see Gerald Graff, *Professing Literature: An Institutional History* (Chicago, 1987).

assumptions on which they had rested no longer enjoyed an easy dominance in the world about them. Added to this, the cultural diversity of American society and the market principles governing individual success in American academic life have helped to make that congeries of second-order reflection now known as 'theory' the central intellectual arena in which reputations are made and battles about power and status are fought out. Focussing on this institutional setting may not go very far towards explaining the actual content of the positions taken up in such debates, but it is indispensable if one is to understand either the apparent disproportion of passion to outcome, or the degree of attention accorded debate on such arcane matters by the wider society.

This points towards the second of the large-scale developments which have thrown a burden of significance onto debates about interpretation, namely the way in which a body of writing rooted in the distinctive preoccupations and manners of proceeding of Continental European philosophy has collided with (any verb suggesting greater mutual understanding or good-will would culpably misrepresent the nature of the encounter) a largely Anglo-Saxon tradition of the critical explication and appreciation of literary works. This development, too, needs to be seen in a longer historical perspective. A defining passage in the unsteady path towards professionalization pursued by literary studies in Britain and America in the course of the twentieth century occurred when the concentration on historical scholarship *about* literature, which had been the legacy of the nineteenth-century attempt to live up to the prevailing conception of 'scientific method', was challenged and very considerably displaced by a critical practice which dwelt with fierce attentiveness on the verbal details of canonical works of 'great literature', a practice associated in Britain with the work of I.A. Richards in 'Practical Criticism' (and in more complicated or remote ways with the critical work of T.S. Eliot, F.R. Leavis, and William Empson), and in the United States with that of the 'New Critics', notably John Crowe Ransom, R.P. Blackmur, Robert Penn Warren, Allen Tate, Cleanth Brooks, and W.K. Wimsatt. This practice eventually generated its own set of justifying doctrines, especially in the United States, at the heart of which was a conception of the work of literature as an aesthetic object – free-standing, autotelic, the dynamics of whose self-sufficient meaning it was the task of the critic to elucidate. A secondary doctrine, derived from this primary dogma, was the repudiation of the so-called 'intentionalist fallacy', the supposed mistake of believing that evidence about the author's pre-textual intentions might be relevant to establishing the 'meaning' of the 'verbal icon' (to use Wimsatt's phrase) that was the work of literature. (In principle, these doctrines were supposed to apply to all literary genres, but it has long been apparent that they were largely developed out of the criticism of, and always least awkwardly referred to, short lyric poetry which abounded in the kinds of 'tensions' and 'ambiguities' whose identification was the particular forte of the leading New Critics.)

The attitudes towards literature and its criticism encouraged by this movement, and which came to have a preponderant though perhaps never monopolistic position in Anglo-American literature departments by the 1950s and 1960s, proved predictably unreceptive to the heterodox ideas about meaning developed within Continental European philosophical traditions, stemming particularly from hermeneutics, phenomenology and structural linguistics. The extension of some of the fundamental ideas of Saussure's linguistic theories, in particular, and their partial congruence with the anthropological theories of Lévi-Strauss, led to the spread across many fields of enquiry from the late 1950s onwards of a search for deep structures and recurrent patterns underlying all areas of human activity. When combined with the revived post-Kantian legacy of the transcendental enquiry into the conditions of the possibility of an activity, this issued in the elaboration of very general theories about the nature of meaning, communication, and similar topics. (The semiology, or science of signs, with which Eco himself has been closely associated, formed part of this larger tendency, pursued at least as much by those trained in philosophy and the social sciences as by those whose allegiances were primarily to the study of literature.) The description of a further instalment of such theorizing as 'poststructuralist' is partly just journalism's need for labels, but it does also suggest how Saussure's insistence on the arbitrariness of the signifier has been the starting point for more recent claims, advanced with dazzling virtuosity by Jacques Derrida in particular, about the instability of all meaning in writing.

The upshot of the spread among those employed to teach literature in British and American universities of enthusiasm for ideas derived from this not always well understood cluster of philosophical traditions has been heated, confused, and by now rather protracted controversy about the whole nature and purpose of literary studies. In the course of this debate, the idea that the establishment of 'the meaning' of a literary text might be a legitimate goal of critical enquiry has come in for some pretty rough handling. The attempt to limit the range of relevant meaning-conferring contexts or to halt the endlessly self-dissolving instabilities of writing has been stigmatized as 'authoritarian' – a charge which is itself an example of the readiness with which complex theoretical questions have been linked to wider political attitudes. Conversely, those wary of what they see as a too easy movement between different levels of abstraction argue that the point of the Derridean denial of epistemic 'certainty' was dependent upon a tradition of post-Cartesian philosophy and should not be taken to cast doubt upon the possibility of establishing conventionally agreed meanings for written texts of all kinds. They support their point by accusing the poststructuralist critic of 'playing a double game, introducing his own interpretive strategy when reading someone else's text, but tacitly relying on communal norms when undertaking to communicate the methods and results of his interpretations to his own readers'.[2]

In choosing the present topic for his lectures, therefore, Eco was committing himself to staking out a position in a fast-moving international discussion, or group of related discussions, about the nature of meaning and the possibilities and limits of interpretation. Having been one of the most influential in drawing attention, in the 1960s and 1970s, to the role of the reader in the process of 'producing' meaning, he has, in his most recent work, expressed an unease at the way some of the leading strands of contemporary critical thought, especially that style of Derrida-inspired American criticism calling itself 'Deconstruction' and associated above all with the work of Paul de Man and J. Hillis Miller, appear to him to licence the reader to produce a limitless, uncheckable flow of 'readings'.[3] Developing this protest against what he sees as the perverse appropriation of the idea of 'unlimited semiosis', Eco's lectures in this volume explore ways of limiting the range of admissable interpretations and hence of identifying certain readings as 'overinterpretation'.

To this end, the first lecture recounts the long history in

---

[2] M.H. Abrams, 'How to do things with texts', in his *Doing Things with Texts: Essays in Criticism and Critical Theory* (New York, 1989), p. 295.

[3] See in particular the pieces gathered in Umberto Eco, *The Limits of Interpretation* (forthcoming).

Western thought of ideas of 'secret' meanings, encoded in language in ways which escape the attention of all but the initiated few. The thrust of this account is to make contemporary theory seem to be a replay of long familiar moves, almost a further stage in the tortuous history of Hermeticism and Gnosticism, in which the more esoteric a form of knowledge can be shown to be the more greatly it is prized, and in which each peeled layer or decoded secret turns out to be but the antechamber to a yet more cunningly concealed truth. A common psychological element in these traditions of interpretation lies in the attitude of suspicion or disdain towards apparent meaning, its very accessibility and seeming concordance with common sense fatally damning its status in the eyes of the Followers of the Veil.

In his second lecture, Eco distances himself still further from the modern form of this tendency by insisting that we can, and do, recognize overinterpretation of a text without necessarily being able to prove that one interpretation is the right one, or even clinging to any belief that there must be *one* right reading. His argument here is chiefly carried by his amusing exploitation of examples, notably of the obsessively Rosicrucian reading of Dante by the relatively obscure nineteenth-century Anglo-Italian man of letters, Gabriele Rossetti. Eco's discussion, in the same spirit, of the interpretation of a Wordsworth poem by the American critic Geoffrey Hartman is intended to indicate another way of exceeding the bounds of legitimate interpretation, though here there may be more readers prepared to find Hartman's reading illuminating rather than exaggerated. In this argument the provocative notion of *intentio operis*, the intention of the work, plays an important role, as a source of meaning which, while not being reducible to the pre-textual *intentio auctoris*, none the less operates as a constraint upon the free play of the *intentio lectoris*. The nature,

9

status, and identification of this *intentio operis* all seem to call for further elaboration, although, drawing upon his own earlier distinctions between the Empirical Reader, the Implied Reader, and the Model Reader, Eco ingeniously construes the notion to suggest that the aim of the text must be to produce the Model Reader – that is to say, the reader who reads it as it is in some sense designed to be read, where that may include the possibility of being read so as to yield multiple interpretations.

Eco's third lecture addresses the related question of whether the Empirical Author has any privileged position as interpreter of 'his' text (a possessive that not all theorists of interpretation would wish to let pass unchallenged). Eco accepts the doctrine, enshrined by the New Critics several decades ago, that the author's pre-textual intention – the purposes that may have led to the attempt to write a particular work – cannot furnish the touchstone of interpretation, and may even be irrelevant or misleading as guides to a text's meaning or meanings. Yet he does argue that, retrospectively, the Empirical Author must be allowed to rule out certain interpretations, although whether they are ruled out as interpretations of what he intended to mean or of what, under any intelligible or persuasive reading, the text could legitimately be made to mean, is less clear. He gives the argument a characteristically personal twist by offering some engaging revelations about the Empirical Author of *The Name of the Rose*, an Empirical Author who in this case, at least, seems also to lay some claim to be the Model Reader.

The papers by the three seminarists each represent responses to Eco's claims grounded in other intellectual traditions and ultimately in different, though at various points interlocking, sets of pre-occupations.

For the past two decades, Richard Rorty ('the most interesting philosopher in the world today' in the opinion of the American critic Harold Bloom) has conducted a forceful and eloquent campaign to persuade us to abandon the foundationalist aspiration at the heart of the Western epistemological tradition.[4] We should no longer, argues Rorty, think of philosophy as the enquiry into The Way Things Really Are, as an attempt to 'mirror' nature, and hence as the basis of all other disciplines, but rather as simply one among several contributions to a continuing cultural conversation in which various vocabularies, various preferred descriptions, recommend themselves to us in so far as they suit our purposes. Rorty has thus developed his own version of the Pragmatism associated with earlier American philosophers like William James and John Dewey, in which we are enjoined rather to think of our concepts as tools we employ for certain purposes rather than as bits of a jig-saw which represent How the World Really Is.

In his comment on Eco, Rorty accordingly takes issue with the distinction between the 'interpretation' of a text and its 'use'. He sees Eco as clinging to the notion that a text has a 'nature' and that legitimate interpretation involves attempting in some way to illuminate that nature, whereas Rorty urges us to forget the idea of discovering What the Text Is Really Like, and instead to think of the various descriptions which we find it useful, for our various purposes, to give. A noticeable feature of Rorty's larger campaign has been the way in which he has redescribed a whole range of conventional theoretical issues in what he would call his own 'preferred final vocabulary', thereby instantiating his belief that intellectual change takes place by people coming to find it more useful, rewarding, or interesting to inhabit a new vocabulary rather than by means of a point-by-point refutation of the earlier view (which, in any

---

4 Some of the major landmarks in this campaign have been 'The world well lost', *Journal of Philosophy*, 69 (1972); *Philosophy and the Mirror of Nature* (Princeton, 1979); *Consequences of Pragmatism (Essays: 1972–1980)* (Minneapolis, 1982); *Contingency, Irony, and Solidarity* (Cambridge, 1989).

event, to function effectively as a refutation of *that* view would have to appeal to the criteria acknowledged in the existing vocabulary). This frequently leads him to announce, with a studied off-handedness that some find exhilarating and others infuriating, that a large number of time-honoured questions just are not interesting questions any more. In the present case, Rorty raises the stakes (and, as it turned out, the temperature too) by announcing that enquiries into 'how texts work' were among these mistaken or unrewarding exercises that we, as cheerful pragmatists, could now abandon. We should simply get on with using texts for our own purposes (which is, in his view, all we can do with them anyway).

At the same time, Rorty does not seem entirely willing to allow that all purposes and all texts are equal, for he prizes those texts which 'will help you change your purposes, and thus to change your life'(106). Towards the end of his paper, he paints an attractive picture of a form of criticism which does not just process all it reads through its established, unyielding conceptual grid, but which is, rather, 'the result of an encounter with an author, character, plot, stanza, line, or archaic torso which has made a difference to the critic's conception of who she is, what she is good for, what she wants to do with herself; an encounter which has re-arranged her priorities and purposes'(107). An inspiriting charter for the role of 'great literature' may seem to be lurking here, but it remains somewhat tantalizing to know how things which have no 'nature' of their own but are merely described in ways which suit our purposes can, on occasion, offer resistance to those purposes, resistance so strong that it succeeds in re-arranging the reader's priorities and purposes.

Jonathan Culler's paper takes issue with both Eco and Rorty. In the meta-literary disputes which have attracted so much attention in academic literary studies in North America in recent years, Culler has been a prominent expounder and to some extent defender of several of the new approaches which are collectively labelled (not always helpfully) 'theory'.[5] In this vein, his paper defends what Eco attacks as 'overinterpretation' (while making the shrewd observation that Eco's extensive writings, both critical and fictional, suggest a recurring fascination with precisely that hermetic, obsessive, search for secret codes that he criticizes in his lectures). Some of what Eco stigmatizes under this name, he suggests, might be better seen as *under*interpretation. But more broadly, Culler is not willing to let the text determine the range of questions we put to it: there can always be interesting questions about what it does *not* say, and the range of what it may come to us to find interesting here cannot be limited in advance. Against Eco's attack that Deconstruction exploits the notion of 'unlimited semiosis' (and hence licences 'arbitrary' interpretations), Culler contends that it acknowledges that meaning is context-bound (and hence not, in any given context, limitless), but that what may count as a fruitful context cannot be specified in advance – that context itself is, in principle, limitless.

Moreover, Culler urges that theoretical reflection upon how in general texts work – how narratives achieve their effects, for example, or how genre determines expectations – can be one very fruitful source of new questions. It is for this reason, above all, that Culler is not willing to accept Rorty's injunction that we should just get on with happily 'using' a text and not worry too much about the mechanics of how it means. Indeed, Culler contends that 'the idea of literary study as a discipline is precisely the attempt to develop a systematic understanding of the semiotic mechanisms of literature' (117). This draws atten-

---

5   See particularly *Structuralist Poetics* (Ithaca, NY, 1975); *On Deconstruction: Theory and Criticism After Structuralism* (Ithaca, NY, 1982); and *Framing the Sign: Criticism and its Institutions* (Norman, OK, 1988).

tion to a form of enquiry Rorty's pragmatist critic seems to undervalue, though the assertion that this is what 'literary study as a discipline' consists in would hardly meet with approval from all those who think of themselves as engaged in that discipline, and is a reminder of why such claims have proved to be so vexed and contentious professionally. Culler also touches on a further issue that can lead to raised voices in the corridor or seminar-room when he suggests that the recommendation by pragmatists like Rorty or Stanley Fish that we simply stop asking certain sorts of questions amounts to kicking away the ladder on which they have mounted to professional success, thereby denying its use to the next generation. Culler wants to see such theoretical questions becoming more not less central to academic literary study, and to that end he urges us to cultivate a 'state of wonder at the play of texts and interpretation'(123). The ultimate justification for such enquiries still appears to be their likely fruitfulness in stimulating new 'discoveries' about texts; what Culler is not willing to allow is any notion of an *intentio operis* which would, by stigmatizing certain readings as 'overinterpretations', limit in advance the range of such potential discoveries.

Christine Brooke-Rose addresses not so much these theoretical questions as others about the nature and purposes served by the genre to which Eco's own fictions belong, and which she calls 'palimpsest history'. As both novelist and critic, she has herself explored, and extended the range of, Modernist and Postmodernist narrative possibilities, always challenging any tendency to return to unilinear Realism as the norm or standard.[6] In her paper, she begins by classifying some of the

---

[6] See *The Christine Brooke-Rose Omnibus: Four Novels* (Manchester, 1986), *Amalgamemnon* (Manchester, 1984), and *Xorander* (Manchester, 1986); her major critical essays to date were collected in *A Rhetoric of the Unreal: Studies in Narrative and Structure, Especially of the Fantastic* (Cambridge, 1981).

ways by which modern fiction has attempted to use or re-work history, transposing modalities of time as well as place to create alternative versions of a collective, and in some cases a self-consciously national, past. Her discussion focusses on the work of Salman Rushdie, but broadens out to suggest that the style of fiction often dubbed 'magic realism', and which she wishes to re-classify as 'palimpsest history', is particularly suited in the age of film and television to doing 'things which only the novel can do' and thus 'to stretch our intellectual, spiritual, and imaginative horizons to breaking-point'(137).

The lively discussion which followed the delivery of the original versions of these papers was dominated by resistance to Rorty's forceful statement of the Pragmatist case. In part, this was a response to the provoking and apparently casual manner in which Rorty consigned various cherished intellectual projects to history's rubbish-bin. For example, when, in contesting Eco's notion of an '*intentio operis*' as a control on the otherwise unlimited diversity of interpretations offered by readers, Rorty says that in his view 'a text just has whatever coherence it happened to acquire during the last roll of the hermeneutic wheel'(97), the laid-backness is intended to sideline more ponderous or portentous vocabularies, but the deliberately nonchalant 'just happen' seems to beg precisely the questions which interest non-Rortians. Several speakers wanted to re-instate the distinction between interpretation and use, or to question how, for the consistent pragmatist, the text could ever offer any resistance to a particular pre-existing use, and hence why literature might be, as Rorty seemed to want it to be, of any special significance. The notion of what is or is not 'interesting' was felt by others to be too problematic to serve as any kind of useful criterion. The novelist–critics present, such as Malcolm Bradbury and David Lodge, evidently sympathized with Eco's desire to limit the range of acceptable interpretation, suggesting that the working practice of the writer clearly presupposed some such limits, some reason for the work being written this way and not that. But this in turn provoked further discussion of the thorny questions raised by the fact of some readers being undeniably more 'competent' than others, and hence of whether we can speak on one 'community of readers', especially where successful works of fiction enjoy wide popular readership. Discussion promised to be as hard to limit as some wished interpretation to be, but time once again proved to be a less tractable medium than writing.

In his reply to the discussion, included here, Eco re-affirms, against the contrasting arguments of both Rorty and Culler, that the properties of the text itself do set limits to the range of legitimate interpretation. He does not appear to maintain that there are any formal criteria by which these limits can be established in theoretical terms, but he invokes instead a kind of cultural Darwinism: certain readings prove themselves over time to the satisfaction of the relevant community. He also points to the way that all the discussants, whatever their explicit theoretical allegiance, in practice look for some kind of unity of belief and sensibility behind the various texts written by a single author, and in line with this he allows himself to speak with some authority on the meaning of those pieces of writing known as *The Name of the Rose* and *Foucault's Pendulum* as well as those which will henceforth be known as his Tanner lectures on *Interpretation and Overinterpretation*.

III

Thirty years ago, reflecting on his own practice as a teacher of modern literature, Lionel Trilling observed that

since my own interests lead me to see literary situations as cultural situations, and cultural situations as great elaborate fights about moral issues, and moral issues as having something to do with gratuitously chosen images of personal being, and images of personal being as having something to do with literary style, I felt free to begin with what for me was a first concern, the animus of the author, the objects of his will, the things he wants or wants to have happen.[7]

The controversies which have dominated literary studies in the three decades since this was written have conspired to call into doubt almost all of Trilling's assumptions, and at first sight the passage may seem to wear its datedness as unmistakably as do the cars and clothes of the same vintage. (The idiosyncrasy of Trilling's quasi-Existentialist view of moral issues as 'having something to do with gratuitously chosen images of personal being', though it might not have been shared by most of his contemporaries, now seems undeniably 'in period'.) And yet, allowing for differences of idiom and reference, the recent debates about interpretation (of which the pieces gathered in this volume form a part) reveal that the connections between 'cultural situations', 'moral issues', 'images of personal being', and 'literary style' are still at work in shaping even the most determinedly theoretical positions. This contention may be briefly illustrated even from those contributions that initially seem least supportive of it.

In Richard Rorty's 'The pragmatist's progress', as in his recent work more generally, his own style very skilfully embodies the larger intellectual and moral attitudes he is recommending. His self-consciously pragmatist cultivation of an informal, homely, American idiom is intended to undercut more portentous vocabularies, and to return human purposes to the centre of the stage. His deliberately voluntarist formulations exemplify his view that we choose between various final

[7] Lionel Trilling, 'On the teaching of modern literature', first published (as 'On the modern element in modern literature') in *Partisan Review* (1961) and repr. in Lionel Trilling, *Beyond Culture: Essays on Literature and Learning* (New York, 1965), p. 13.

vocabularies: thus, he frequently writes 'I would prefer to say x' or 'we pragmatists wish that de Man had not done y' instead of some more conventional claims that 'x is the case' or 'de Man was mistaken in doing y', just as he refers to 'my own favourite philosophy of language' rather than stating the case in any terms tainted by residual foundationalism. He uses the first-person plural with almost incantatory frequency – 'what we are interested in', 'we pragmatists', 'we Davidsonians and we Fishians' – though here the foregrounding of the human bearers of the views in question teeters on the edge of a collusive chumminess. And, as I have already remarked, faced with the constantly re-iterated claim that the point or value of any activity or enquiry depends simply upon 'what we are interested in', we (a community of non-Rortian readers, perhaps) may feel we want to know rather more about what shapes this notion of 'interesting', or more about the grounds on which we could begin to adjudicate among conflicting claims on our interest.

The Implied Pragmatist in Rorty's account may talk in a homely idiom, but she also entertains large ambitions of self-creation. This ambition is alluded to in his discussion of the distinction between 'knowing what you want to get out of a thing or person in advance' and 'hoping that the person or thing or text will help you to change your purposes, and thus to change your life'(106). A certain 'image of personal being' is implicit here, as it is in his giving pride of place to that encounter with a text by which the reader is 'enraptured or destabilized'(107). Elsewhere, Rorty has spoken favourably of an idea of philosophy that 'might change our lives, rather than grounding our customs and guaranteeing our habits',[8] and at

---

[8] Richard Rorty, 'Philosophy and post-modernism', *The Cambridge Review*, 110 (1989), 52.

work here is the same urge to make it new, to be perpetually recreating oneself – an urge that can be given a classy (as Rorty would characteristically say) intellectual genealogy going back to Nietzsche, but which more obviously has an affinity with that more everyday American belief in the possibility of escaping the constraints of history, whether collective or personal. The attendant 'can-do' briskness can express an impatience with the intractable material of intellectual tradition no less than of social structure. For all the brilliance of his anti-philosophical polemics and the thought-provoking range of his cultural criticism, there is a strain in Rorty's anti-essentialism that may seem to encourage a kind of anti-intellectualism. The range of questions which 'we pragmatists' would say there is no point in asking threatens to shrink the horizons of intellectual enquiry. As both Eco and Culler point out, there may be a quite legitimate interest in 'how language works', or 'how texts work', an interest which, thus expressed, Rorty would presumably not deny, but which may seem to be treated too dismissively by his quickly moving to insist that such enquiries cannot 'tell you anything about the nature of texts or the nature of reading. For neither has a nature' (105).

Culler's paper, for all its crisp and well-informed professionalism, also intimates a set of preferred attitudes. A willingness, perhaps even an obligation, to embrace novelty; a commitment to challenging whatever the well-established cherish or take for granted; an alertness to the play of power and authority both in the academic profession and in society more generally – these are not insignificant human values. They also express a sense of identity in which an awareness of one's intellectual and political credentials, of 'taking a position', is prominent. When, for example, Culler asserts that 'like most activities, interpretation is interesting only when it is extreme'(110), the provokingly general form of the statement asks to be given credit for a willingness, and capacity, to express a Nietzschean irreverence towards the sensible pieties of the academic world (while perhaps running the risk of seeming to invoke a thinly adolescent notion of what counts as 'interesting').

Fittingly, it is Culler who explicitly introduces the topic of 'the profession' in his complaint about Rorty's ladder-kicking. For, his linking of a defence of 'overinterpretation' with his concern about how 'the young or marginalized could challenge the views of those who currently occupy positions of authority in literary studies'(119) will surely speak to the dilemma faced by those ambitious to make a career in the professional study of literature, above all in the competitive and fashion-conscious market of American academic life. Succinctly expressed, the dilemma is that the traditionally canonical works of literature have by now been very thoroughly studied. An essential condition of launching a successful and high-profile professional career is the promotion of some striking novelty; mere intelligent endorsement of the more persuasive of the available interpretations of major works is not enough. Much non-canonical material beckons, promising near-virgin lands for the rearing of a good crop of new interpretations, just as various other historical and editorial tasks propose themselves as requiring the labour of the coming generation. But the risk, for the young scholar with eyes fixed on the rapid establishment of a glittering reputation, is that these will be classed as minor or marginal achievements: attention is gained, and work of acknowledged significance performed, by offering fresh interpretations of works which are indisputably central. Novelty, or at least apparent novelty, of method and provocativeness of formulation are, therefore, at a premium (quite apart from all the other intellectual impulsions to extend the range of understanding). Culler himself, both in his paper here and in his lucid expositions of recent critical trends, provides a principled defence of the case for new readings and of the variety of intellectual strategies that may help to provoke them; but at the same time the terms in which he characterizes the present 'cultural situation' (to take up Trilling's terms once more) inevitably secrete a further 'image of personal being'.

There will be those, of course, who will dismiss all talk of 'moral issues' and 'images of personal being' as irredeemably 'humanist', the legacy of a now discredited set of assumptions about the givenness of the pre-linguistic knowing subject. However, not only are the terms of that description itself still very much a matter of debate, but all attempts to deploy a persuasive 'post-humanist' vocabulary unavoidably express attitudes towards human experience that can only be called ethical. Even a preference for 'openness of meaning' rather than 'authoritarian interpretation', and still more any attendant recommendation of 'endless self-fashioning' as against 'conformist essentialism', appeals to some scale of evaluation, however implicit. But to point this out is only to point to further ways of continuing the argument, not an attempt to conclude it. It also suggests that our anxious committee-member need not have worried: as the striking vitality and diversity of the contributions to this volume amply testify, the issue of interpretation and overinterpretation touches questions of 'human values' at every point.

I

Interpretation and history

UMBERTO ECO

In 1957 J.M. Castillet wrote a book entitled *La hora del lector* ('The hour of the reader').[1] He was indeed a prophet. In 1962 I wrote my *Opera aperta*.[2] In that book I advocated the active role of the interpreter in the reading of texts endowed with aesthetic value. When those pages were written, my readers mainly focussed on the open side of the whole business, underestimating the fact that the open-ended reading I was supporting was an activity elicited by (and aiming at interpreting) a work. In other words, I was studying the dialectics between the rights of texts and the rights of their interpreters. I have the impression that, in the course of the last decades, the rights of the interpreters have been overstressed.

In my more recent writings (*A Theory of Semiotics*, *The Role of the Reader*, and *Semiotics and the Philosophy of Language*)[3] I elaborated on the Peircean idea of unlimited semiosis. In my presentation at the Peirce International Congress at Harvard University (September 1989) I tried to show that the notion of unlimited semiosis does not lead to the conclusion that interpretation has no criteria. To say that interpretation (as the

[1] J.M. Castillet, *La hora del lector* (Barcelona, 1957).
[2] Translated as *The Open Work* (Cambridge, MA, 1989).
[3] All published by Indiana University Press in, respectively, 1976, 1979 and 1984.

basic feature of semiosis) is potentially unlimited does not mean that interpretation has no object and that it 'riverruns' merely for its own sake.[4] To say that a text has potentially no end does not mean that every act of interpretation can have a happy end.

Some contemporary theories of criticism assert that the only reliable reading of a text is a misreading, that the only existence of a text is given by the chain of responses it elicits, and that, as maliciously suggested by Todorov (quoting Lichtenberg à propos of Boehme), a text is only a picnic where the author brings the words and the readers bring the sense.[5]

Even if that were true, the words brought by the author are a rather embarrassing bunch of material evidences that the reader cannot pass over in silence, or in noise. If I remember correctly, it was here in Britain that somebody suggested, years ago, that it is possible to do things with words. To interpret a text means to explain why these words can do various things (and not others) through the way they are interpreted. But if Jack the Ripper told us that he did what he did on the grounds of his interpretation of the Gospel according to Saint Luke, I suspect that many reader-oriented critics would be inclined to think that he read Saint Luke in a pretty preposterous way. Non-reader-oriented critics would say that Jack the Ripper was deadly mad – and I confess that, even though feeling very sympathetic with the reader-oriented paradigm, and even though I have read Cooper, Laing, and Guattari, much to my regret I would agree that Jack the Ripper needed medical care.

I understand that my example is rather far-fetched and that even the most radical deconstructionist would agree (I hope, but who knows?) with me. Nevertheless, I think that even such a paradoxical argument must be taken seriously. It proves that there is at least one case in which it is possible to say that a

---

[4] See now Umberto Eco, *The Limits of Interpretation* (forthcoming).
[5] T. Todorov, 'Viaggio nella critica americana', *Lettera*, 4 (1987), 12.

given interpretation is a bad one. In terms of Popper's theory of scientific research, this is enough to disprove the hypothesis that interpretation has no public criteria (at least statistically speaking).

One could object that the only alternative to a radical reader-oriented theory of interpretation is the one extolled by those who say that the only valid interpretation aims at finding the original intention of the author. In some of my recent writings I have suggested that between the intention of the author (very difficult to find out and frequently irrelevant for the interpretation of a text) and the intention of the interpreter who (to quote Richard Rorty) simply 'beats the text into a shape which will serve for his purpose', there is a third possibility.[6] There is an *intention of the text*.

In the course of my second and third lectures I shall try to make clear what I mean by intention of the text (or *intentio operis*, as opposed to – or interacting with – the *intentio auctoris* and the *intentio lectoris*). In this lecture I would like, by contrast, to revisit the archaic roots of the contemporary debate on the meaning (or the plurality of meanings, or the absence of any transcendental meaning) of a text. Let me, for the moment, blur the distinction between literary and everyday texts, as well as the difference between texts as images of the world and the natural world as (according to a venerable tradition) a Great Text to be deciphered.

Let me, for the moment, start an archaeological trip which, at first glance, would lead us very far away from contemporary theories of textual interpretation. You will see at the end that, on the contrary, most so-called 'post-modern' thought will look very pre-antique.

In 1987 I was invited by the directors of the Frankfurt Book

---

6 Richard Rorty, *Consequences of Pragmatism* (Minneapolis, University of Minnesota Press, 1982), p. 151.

Fair to give an introductory lecture, and the directors of the Book Fair proposed to me (probably believing that this was a really up-to-date subject) a reflection on modern irrationalism. I started by remarking that it is difficult to define 'irrationalism' without having some philosophical concept of 'reason'. Unfortunately, the whole history of Western philosophy serves to prove that such a definition is rather controversial. Any way of thinking is always seen as irrational by the historical model of another way of thinking, which views itself as rational. Aristotle's logic is not the same as Hegel's; *Ratio, Ragione, Raison, Reason* and *Vernunft* do not mean the same thing.

One way of understanding philosophical concepts is often to come back to the common sense of dictionaries. In German I find that the synonyms of 'irrational' are '*unsinnig, unlogisch, unvernünftig, sinnlos*'; in English they are 'senseless, absurd, nonsensical, incoherent, delirious, farfetched, inconsequential, disconnected, illogic, exorbitant, extravagant, skimble-skamble'. These meanings seem too much or too little for defining respectable philosophical standpoints. None the less, all these terms indicate something going beyond a limit set by a standard. One of the antonyms of 'unreasonableness' (according to *Roget's Thesaurus*) is 'moderateness'. Being moderate means being within the *modus* – that is, within limits and within measure. The word reminds us of two rules we have inherited from the ancient Greek and Latin civilizations: the logical principle of *modus ponens* and the ethical principle formulated by Horace: *est modus in rebus, sunt certi denique fines quos ultra citraque nequit consistere rectum.*[7]

At this point I understand that the Latin notion of *modus* was rather important, if not for determining the difference between rationalism and irrationalism, at least for isolating two basic

---

[7] Horace, *Satires* I.I.106–7.

interpretative attitudes, that is, two ways of deciphering either a text as a world or the world as a text. For Greek rationalism, from Plato to Aristotle and others, knowledge meant understanding causes. In this way, defining God meant defining a cause, beyond which there could be no further cause. To be able to define the world in terms of causes, it is essential to develop the idea of a unilinear chain: if a movement goes from A to B, then there is no force on earth that will be able to make it go from B to A. In order to be able to justify the unilinear nature of the causal chain, it is first necessary to assume a number of principles: the principle of identity ($A = A$), the principle of non-contradiction (it is impossible for something both to be A and not to be A at the same time) and the principle of the excluded middle (either A is true or A is false and *tertium non datur*). From these principles we derive the typical pattern of thinking of Western rationalism, the *modus ponens*: 'if p then q; but p: therefore q'.

Even if these principles do not provide for the recognition of a physical order to the world, they do at least provide a social contract. Latin rationalism adopts the principles of Greek rationalism but transforms and enriches them in a legal and contractual sense. The legal standard is *modus*, but the *modus* is also the limit, the boundaries.

The Latin obsession with spatial limits goes right back to the legend of the foundation of Rome: Romulus draws a boundary line and kills his brother for failing to respect it. If boundaries are not recognized, then there can be no *civitas*. Horatius becomes a hero because he manages to hold the enemy on the border – a bridge thrown up between the Romans and the Others. Bridges are sacrilegious because they span the *sulcus*, the moat of water delineating the city boundaries: for this reason, they may be built only under the close, ritual control of the Pontifex. The ideology of the Pax Romana and Caesar

Augustus's political design are based on a precise definition of boundaries: the force of the empire is in knowing on which borderline, between which *limen* or threshold, the defensive line should be set up. If the time ever comes when there is no longer a clear definition of boundaries, and the barbarians (nomads who have abandoned their original territory and who move about on any territory as if it were their own, ready to abandon that too) succeed in imposing their nomadic view, then Rome will be finished and the capital of the empire could just as well be somewhere else.

Julius Caesar, in crossing the Rubicon, not only knows that he is committing sacrilege but knows that, once he has committed it, then can never turn back. *Alea iacta est*. In point of fact, there are also limits in time. What has been done can never be erased. Time is irreversible. This principle was to govern Latin syntax. The direction and sequence of tenses, which is cosmological linearity, makes itself a system of logical subordinations in the *consecutio temporum*. That masterpiece of factual realism which is the absolute ablative establishes that, once something has been done, or presupposed, then it may never again be called into question.

In a *Quaestio quodlibetalis*, Thomas Aquinas (5.2.3) wonders whether *'utrum Deus possit virginem reparare'* – in other words, whether a woman who has lost her virginity can be returned to her original undefiled condition. Thomas's answer is clear. God may forgive and thus return the virgin to a state of grace and may, by performing a miracle, give back her bodily integrity. But even God cannot cause what has been not to have been, because such a violation of the laws of time would be contrary to his very nature. God cannot violate the logical principle whereby 'p has occurred' and 'p has not occurred' would appear to be in contradiction. *Alea iacta est*.

This model of Greek and Latin rationalism is the one that still dominates mathematics, logic, science, and computer programming. But it is not the whole story of what we call the Greek legacy. Aristotle was Greek but so were the Eleusinian mysteries. The Greek world is continuously attracted by *Apeiron* (infinity). Infinity is that which has no *modus*. It escapes the norm. Fascinated by infinity, Greek civilization, alongside the concept of identity and noncontradiction, constructs the idea of continuous metamorphosis, symbolized by Hermes. Hermes is volatile and ambiguous, he is father of all the arts but also God of robbers – *iuvenis et senex* at the same time. In the myth of Hermes we find the negation of the principle of identity, of non-contradiction, and of the excluded middle, and the causal chains wind back on themselves in spirals: the 'after' precedes the 'before', the god knows no spatial limits and may, in different shapes, be in different places at the same time.

Hermes is triumphant in the second century after Christ. The second century is a period of political order and peace, and all the peoples of the empire are apparently united by a common language and culture. The order is such that no one can any longer hope to change it with any form of military or political operation. It is the time when the concept of *enkyklios paideia*, of general education, is defined, the aim of which is to produce a type of complete man, versed in all the disciplines. This knowledge, however, describes a perfect, coherent world, whereas the world of the second century is a melting-pot of races and languages; a crossroad of peoples and ideas, one where all gods are tolerated. These gods had formerly had a deep meaning for the people worshipping them, but when the empire swallowed up their countries, it also dissolved their identity: there are no longer any differences between Isis, Astartes, Demetra, Cybele, Anaitis, and Maia.

We have all heard the legend of the Caliph who ordered the

destruction of the library of Alexandria, arguing that either the books said the same thing as the Koran, in which case they were superfluous, or else they said something different, in which case they were wrong and harmful. The Caliph knew and possessed the truth and he judged the books on the basis of that truth. Second-century Hermetism, on the other hand, is looking for a truth it does not know, and all it possesses is books. Therefore, it imagines or hopes that each book will contain a spark of truth and that they will serve to confirm each other. In this syncretistic dimension, one of the principles of Greek rationalist models, that of the excluded middle, enters a crisis. It is possible for many things to be true at the same time, even if they contradict each other. But if books tell the truth, even when they contradict each other, then their each and every word must be an allusion, an allegory. They are saying something other than what they appear to be saying. Each one of them contains a message that none of them will ever be able to reveal alone. In order to be able to understand the mysterious message contained in books, it was necessary to look for a revelation beyond human utterances, one which would come announced by divinity itself, using the vehicle of vision, dream, or oracle. But such an unprecedented revelation, never heard before, would have to speak of an as yet unknown god and of a still-secret truth. Secret knowledge is deep knowledge (because only what is lying under the surface can remain unknown for long). Thus truth becomes identified with what is not said or what is said obscurely and must be understood beyond or beneath the surface of a text. The gods speak (today we would say: the Being is speaking) through hieroglyphic and enigmatic messages.

By the way, if the search for a different truth is born of a mistrust of the classical Greek heritage, then any true knowledge will have to be more archaic. It lies among the remains of civilizations that the fathers of Greek rationalism had ignored. Truth is something we have been living with from the beginning of time, except that we have forgotten it. If we have forgotten it, then someone must have saved it for us and it must be someone whose words we are no longer capable of understanding. So this knowledge may be exotic. Jung has explained how it is that once any divine image has become too familiar to us and has lost its mystery, we then need to turn to images of other civilizations, because only exotic symbols are capable of maintaining an aura of sacredness. For the second century, this secret knowledge would thus have been in the hands either of the Druids, the Celtic priests, or wise men from the East, who spoke incomprehensible tongues. Classical rationalism identified barbarians with those who could not even speak properly (that is actually the etymology of *barbaros* – one who stutters). Now, turning things around, it is the supposed stuttering of the foreigner that becomes the sacred language, full of promises and silent revelations. Whereas for Greek rationalism a thing was true if it could be explained, a true thing was now mainly something that could not be explained.

But what was this mysterious knowledge possessed by the barbarians' priests? The widespread opinion was that they knew the secret links that connected the spiritual world to the astral world and the latter to the sub-lunar world, which meant that by acting on a plant it was possible to influence the course of the stars, that the course of the stars affected the fate of the terrestrial beings, and that the magic operations performed about the image of a god would force that god to follow our volition. As here below, so in heaven above. The universe becomes one big hall of mirrors, where any one individual object both reflects and signifies all the others.

It is only possible to speak of universal sympathy and

likeness if, at the same time, the principle of non-contradiction is rejected. Universal sympathy is brought about by a godly emanation in the world, but at the origin of the emanation there is an unknowable One, who is the very seat of the contradiction itself. Neo-platonist Christian thought will try to explain that we cannot define God in clear-cut terms on account of the inadequacy of our language. Hermetic thought states that our language, the more ambiguous and multivalent it is, and the more it uses symbols and metaphors, the more it is particularly appropriate for naming a Oneness in which the coincidence of opposites occurs. But where the coincidence of opposites triumphs, the principle of identity collapses. *Tout se tient.*

As a consequence, interpretation is indefinite. The attempt to look for a final, unattainable meaning leads to the acceptance of a never-ending drift or sliding of meaning. A plant is not defined in terms of its morphological and functional character-istics but on the basis of its resemblance, albeit only partial, to another element in the cosmos. If it is vaguely like part of the human body, then it has meaning because it refers to the body. But that part of the body has meaning because it refers to a star, and the latter has meaning because it refers to a musical scale, and this in turn because it refers to a hierarchy of angels, and so on ad infinitum. Every object, be it earthly or heavenly, hides a secret. Every time a secret has been discovered, it will refer to another secret in a progressive movement toward a final secret. Nevertheless, there can be no final secret. The ultimate secret of Hermetic initiation is that everything is secret. Hence the Hermetic secret must be an empty one, because anyone who pretends to reveal any sort of secret is not himself initiated and has stopped at a superficial level of the knowledge of cosmic mystery. Hermetic thought transforms the whole world theatre into a linguistic phenomenon and at the same time denies language any power of communication.

In the basic texts of the *Corpus Hermeticum*, which appeared in the Mediterranean Basin during the second century, Hermes Trismegistos receives his revelation in the course of a dream or vision, in which the *Nous* appear unto him. For Plato, *Nous* was the faculty that engendered ideas and, for Aristotle, it was the intellect, thanks to which we recognize substances. Certainly, the agility of *Nous* worked counter to the more complicated operations of *dianoia*, which (as early as Plato) was reflection, rational activity; to *episteme*, as a science; and to *phronesis* as a reflection on truth; but there was nothing ineffable in the way it worked. On the contrary, in the second century, *Nous* became the faculty for mystic intuition, for non-rational illumination, and for an instantaneous and non-discursive vision. It is no longer necessary to talk, to discuss, and to reason. We just have to wait for someone to speak for us. Then light will be so fast as to merge with darkness. This is the true initiation of which the initiated may not speak.

If there is no longer temporal linearity ordered in causal links, then the effect may act on its own causes. This actually happens in Theurgical magic but it also happens in philology. The rationalist principle of *post hoc, ergo propter hoc* is replaced with *post hoc, ergo ante hoc*. An example of this type of attitude is the way in which Renaissance thinkers demonstrated that the *Corpus Hermeticum* was not a product of Greek culture but had been written before Plato: the fact that the *Corpus* contains ideas that were obviously in circulation at the time of Plato both means and proves that it appeared before Plato.

If these are the ideas of classical Hermetism, they returned when it celebrated its second victory over the rationalism of medieval scholastics. Throughout the centuries when Christian rationalism was trying to prove the existence of God by means of patterns of reasoning inspired by the *modus ponens*, Hermetic knowledge did not die. It survived, as a marginal phenomenon, among alchemists and Jewish Cabalists and in the folds of the timid medieval Neo-platonism. But, at the dawn of what we call the modern world, in Florence, where in the meantime the modern banking economy was being invented, the *Corpus Hermeticum* – that creation of the second Hellenistic century – was rediscovered as evidence of a very ancient knowledge going back even before Moses. Once it has been reworked by Pico della Mirandola, Ficino, and Johannes Reuchlin, that is to say, by Renaissance Neo-platonism and by Christian Cabalism, the Hermetic model went on to feed a large portion of modern culture, ranging from magic to science.

The history of this rebirth is a complex one: today, historiography has shown us that it is impossible to separate the Hermetic thread from the scientific one or Paracelsus from Galileo. Hermetic knowledge influences Francis Bacon, Copernicus, Kepler, and Newton, and modern quantitative science is born, inter alia, in a dialogue with the qualitative knowledge of Hermetism. In the final analysis, the Hermetic model was suggesting the idea that the order of the universe described by Greek rationalism could be subverted and that it was possible to discover new connections and new relationships in the universe such as would have permitted man to act on nature and change its course. But this influence is merged with the conviction that the world should not be described in terms of a qualitative logic but of a quantitative one. Thus the Hermetic model paradoxically contributes to the birth of its new adversary, modern scientific rationalism. New Hermetic irrationalism oscillates between, on the one hand, mystics and alchemists, and on the other, poets and philosophers, from Goethe to Gérard de Nerval and Yeats, from Schelling to Franz von Baader, from Heidegger to Jung. And in many post-modern concepts of criticism, it is not difficult to recognize the idea of the continuous slippage of meaning. The idea expressed by Paul Valéry, for whom *il n'y a pas de vrai sens d'un texte*, is a Hermetic one.

In one of his books, *Science de l'homme et tradition* – highly questionable for its author's fidestic enthusiasm, though not without alluring arguments – Gilbert Durand sees the whole of contemporary thought, in opposition to the positivist mechanistic paradigm, run through the vivifying breath of Hermes, and the list of relationships he identifies invites reflection: Spengler, Dilthey, Scheler, Nietzsche, Husserl, Kerényi, Planck, Pauli, Oppenheimer, Einstein, Bachelard, Sorokin, Lévi-Strauss, Foucault, Derrida, Barthes, Todorov, Chomsky, Greimas, Deleuze.[8]

But this pattern of thought deviating from the standard of Greek and Latin rationalism would be incomplete if we were to fail to consider another phenomenon taking shape during the same period of history. Dazzled by lightning visions while feeling his way around in the dark, second-century man developed a neurotic awareness of his own role in an incomprehensible world. Truth is secret and any questioning of the symbols and enigmas will never reveal ultimate truth but simply displace the secret elsewhere. If this is the human condition, then it means that the world is the result of a mistake. The cultural expression of this psychological state is Gnosis.

In the tradition of Greek rationalism, Gnosis meant true knowledge of existence (both conversational and dialetic) as opposed to simple perception (*aisthesis*) or opinion (*doxa*). But in the early Christian centuries the word came to mean a meta-rational, intuitive knowledge, the gift, divinely bestowed or received from a celestial intermediary, which has the power to save anyone attaining it. Gnostic revelation tells in a mythical

---

[8]   Gilbert Durand, *Science de l'homme et tradition* (Paris, Berg, 1979).

form how divinity itself, being obscure and unknowable, already contains the germ of evil and an androgyny which makes it contradictory from the very start, since it is not identical to itself. Its subordinate executor, the Demiurge, gives life to an erroneous, instable world, into which a portion of divinity itself falls as if into prison or exile. A world created by mistake is an aborted cosmos. Among the principal effects of this abortion is time, a deformed imitation of eternity. Throughout the same period of centuries, patristics was endeavouring to reconcile Jewish Messianism with Greek rationalism and invented the concept of the providential, rational guidance of history. Gnosticism, on the other hand, developed a rejection syndrome vis-à-vis both time and history.

The Gnostic views himself as an exile in the world, as the victim of his own body, which he defines as a tomb and a prison. He has been cast into the world, from which he must find a way out. Existence is an ill – and we know it. The more frustrated we feel here, the more we are struck with a delirium of omnipotence and desires for revenge. Hence the Gnostic recognizes himself as a spark of divinity, provisionally cast into exile as a result of a cosmic plot. If he manages to return to God, man will not only be reunited with his own beginnings and origin, but will also help to regenerate that very origin and to free it from the original error. Although a prisoner in a sick world, man feels himself invested with superhuman power. Divinity can make amends for its initial breakage thanks only to man's cooperation. Gnostic man becomes an *Übermensch*. By contrast with those that are bound to mere matter (*hylics*), it is only those that are of spirit (*pneumatikoi*) who are able to aspire to truth and hence redemption. Unlike Christianity, Gnosticism is not a religion for slaves but one for masters.

It is difficult to avoid the temptation of seeing a Gnostic inheritance in many aspects of modern and contemporary culture. A Catharic, and hence a Gnostic, origin has been seen in the courteous (and thus romantic) love relationship, seen as a renouncement, as the loss of the loved one, and at all events as a purely spiritual relationship excluding any sexual connection. The aesthetic celebration of evil as a revelationary experience is certainly Gnostic, as is the decision of so many modern poets to search for visionary experiences through exhaustion of the flesh, by means of sexual excess, mystic ecstasy, drugs, and verbal delirium.

Some people have seen a Gnostic root in the governing principles of romantic idealism, where time and history are reassessed, but only to make man the protagonist for the reintegration of the Spirit. On the other hand, when Lukàcs claims that the philosophical irrationalism of the last two centuries is an invention of the bourgeoisie trying to react to the crisis it is facing and giving a philosophical justification to its own will to power and its own imperialistic practice, he is simply translating the Gnostic syndrome into a Marxist language. There are those who have spoken of Gnostic elements in Marxism and even in Leninism (the theory of the party as the spearhead, an elect group possessing the keys to knowledge and hence to redemption). Others see a Gnostic inspiration in existentialism and particularly in Heidegger (existence, Dasein, as being 'cast into the world', the relationship between worldly existence and time, pessimism). Jung, in taking another look at ancient Hermetic doctrines, recast the Gnostic problem in terms of the rediscovery of the original ego. But in the same way a Gnostic element has been identified in every condemnation of mass society by the aristocracy, where the prophets of elected races, in order to bring about the final reintegration of the perfect, have turned to bloodshed, massacre, the genocide of slaves, of those inescapably tied to *hyle*, or matter.

Both together, the Hermetic and the Gnostic heritage produce the syndrome of the secret. If the initiated is someone who understands the cosmic secret, then degenerations of the Hermetic model have led to the conviction that power consists in making others believe that one has a political secret. According to Georg Simmel:

the secret gives one a position of exception; it operates as a purely socially determined attraction. It is basically independent of the context it guards but, of course, is increasingly effective in the measure in which the exclusive possession of it is vast and significant... From secrecy, which shades all that is profound and significant, grows the typical error according to which everything mysterious is something important and essential. Before the unknown, man's natural impulse to idealize and his natural fearfulness cooperate toward the same goal: to intensify the unknown through imagination, and to pay attention to it with an emphasis that is not usually accorded to patent reality.[9]

Let me try now to suggest in which sense the results of our trip toward the roots of the Hermetic legacy can be of some interest for understanding some of the contemporary theory of textual interpretation. Certainly, a common materialistic point of view is not sufficient to draw any connection between Epicurus and Stalin. In the same vein, I doubt that it would be possible to isolate common features between Nietzsche and Chomsky, in spite of Gilbert Durand's celebration of the new Hermetic atmosphere. Still, it can be interesting for the purpose of my lectures to list the main features of what I would like to call a Hermetic approach to texts. We find in ancient

[9] Georg Simmel, 'The secret and the secret society', *The Sociology of Georg Simmel*, trans. and ed. by Kurt H. Wolff (New York, Free Press, 1950), pp. 332–3.

Hermetism and in many contemporary approaches some disquietingly similar ideas: namely, that

A text is an open-ended universe where the interpreter can discover infinite interconnections.

Language is unable to grasp a unique and pre-existing meaning: on the contrary, language's duty is to show that what we can speak of is only the coincidence of the opposites.

Language mirrors the inadequacy of thought: our being-in-the-world is nothing else than being incapable of finding any transcendental meaning.

Any text, pretending to assert something univocal, is a miscarried universe, that is, the work of a muddle-headed Demiurge (who tried to say that 'that's that' and on the contrary elicited an uninterrupted chain of infinite deferrals where 'that' is not 'that').

Contemporary textual Gnosticism is very generous, however: everybody, provided one is eager to impose the intention of the reader upon the unattainable intention of the author, can become the *Übermensch* who really realizes the truth, namely, that the author did not know what he or she was really saying, because language spoke in his or her place.

To salvage the text – that is, to transform it from an illusion of meaning to the awareness that meaning is infinite – the reader must suspect that every line of it conceals another secret meaning; words, instead of saying, hide the untold; the glory of the reader is to discover that texts can say everything, except what their author wanted them to mean; as soon as a pretended meaning is allegedly discovered, we are sure that it is not the real one; the real one is the further one and so on and so forth; the *hylics* – the losers – are those who end the process by saying 'I understood'.

The Real Reader is the one who understands that the secret of a
    text is its emptiness.

I know that I have made a caricature out of the most radical
reader-oriented theories of interpretation. Besides, I think that
caricatures are frequently good portraits: probably not portraits of what is the case, but at least of what could become the
case, if something were assumed to be the case.

What I want to say is that there are somewhere criteria for
limiting interpretation. Otherwise we risk facing a merely
linguistic paradox of the kind formulated by Macedonio
Fernandez: 'In this world there are so many things lacking that,
if there lacked one thing more, there would not be any room for
it.' I know that there are poetic texts whose aim is to show that
interpretation can be infinite. I know that *Finnegans Wake* was
written for an ideal reader affected by an ideal insomnia. But I
also know that although the entire opus of the Marquis de Sade
was written in order to show what sex could be, most of us are
more moderate.

At the beginning of his *Mercury; Or, the Secret and Swift
Messenger* (1641), John Wilkins tells the following story:

How strange a thing this Art of Writing did seem at its first Invention,
we may guess by the late discovered Americans, who were amazed to
see Men converse with Books, and could scarce make themselves to
believe that a Paper could speak. . .

There is a pretty Relation to this Purpose, concerning an Indian
Slave; who being sent by his Master with a Basket of Figs and a Letter,
did by the Way eat up a great Part of his Carriage, conveying the
Remainder unto the Person to whom he was directed; who when he
had read the Letter, and not finding the Quantity of Figs answerable
to what was spoken of, he accuses the Slave of eating them, telling
him what the Letter said against him. But the Indian (notwithstanding this Proof) did confidently abjure the Fact, cursing the Paper, as
being a false and lying Witness.

After this, being sent again with the like Carriage, and a Letter expressing the just Number of Figs, that were to be delivered, he did again, according to his former Practice, devour a great Part of them by the Way; but before he meddled with any, (to prevent all following Accusations) he first took the Letter, and hid that under a great Stone, assuring himself, that if it did not see him eating the Figs, it could never tell of him; but being now more strongly accused than before, he confesses the Fault, admiring the Divinity of the Paper, and for the future does promise his best Fidelity in every Employment.[10]

Someone could say that a text, once it is separated from its utterer (as well as from the utterer's intention) and from the concrete circumstances of its utterance (and by consequence from its intended referent) floats (so to speak) in the vacuum of a potentially infinite range of possible interpretations. Wilkins could have objected that in the case he was reporting, the master was sure that the basket mentioned in the letter was the one carried by the slave, that the carrying slave was exactly the one to whom his friend gave the basket, and that there was a relationship between the expression '30' written in the letter and the number of figs contained in the basket. Naturally, it would be sufficient to imagine that along the way the original slave was killed and another person substituted, that the thirty original figs were replaced with other figs, that the basket was brought to a different addressee, that the new addressee did not know of any friend eager to send him figs. Would it still be possible to decide what the letter was speaking about? We are, nevertheless, entitled to suppose that the reaction of the new addressee would have been of this sort: 'Somebody, and God knows who, sent me a quantity of figs which is lower than the number mentioned in the accompanying letter.' Let us suppose now that not only was the messenger killed but that his killers ate all the figs, destroyed the basket, put the letter into a bottle

[10] John Wilkins, *Mercury; Or, the Secret and Swift Messenger*, 3rd ed. (London, Nicholson, 1707), pp. 3–4.

and threw it in the ocean, so that it was found seventy years after by Robinson Crusoe. No basket, no slave, no figs, only a letter. Notwithstanding this, I bet that the first reaction of Robinson would have been: 'Where are the figs?'

Now, let us suppose that the message in the bottle is found by a more sophisticated person, a student of linguistics, hermeneutics, or semiotics. Being very smart, such a new accidental addressee could make a lot of hypotheses, namely:

1 Figs can be intended (at least today) in a rhetorical sense (as in such expressions as 'to be in good fig', 'to be in full fig', 'to be in poor fig'), and the message could support a different interpretation. But even in this case the addressee will rely upon certain pre-established conventional interpretations of 'fig' which are not those of say, 'apple' or 'cat'.

2 The message in the bottle is an allegory, written by a poet: the addressee smells in that message a hidden second sense based upon a private poetic code, holding only for that text. In this case the addressee could make various conflicting hypotheses, but I strongly believe that there are certain 'economical' criteria on the grounds of which certain hypotheses will be more interesting than others. To validate his or her hypothesis, the addressee probably ought to make certain previous hypotheses about the possible sender and the possible historical period in which the text was produced. This has nothing to do with research about the intentions of the sender, but it has certainly to do with research about the cultural framework of the original message.

Probably our sophisticated interpreter would decide that the text found in the bottle had at one time referred to some existing figs and had indexically pointed toward a given sender as well as toward a given addressee and a given slave, but that now it had lost every referential power. Still, the message will remain a text that one could certainly use for innumerable other baskets and other innumerable figs, but not for apples and unicorns. The addressee can dream of those lost actors, so ambiguously involved in changing things or symbols (perhaps to send figs meant, at a given historical moment, to make an uncanny innuendo), and could start from that anonymous message in order to try a variety of meanings and referents. But he or she would not be entitled to say that the message can mean *everything*. It can mean many things, but there are senses that it would be preposterous to suggest. Certainly, it says that once upon a time there was a basket full of figs. No reader-oriented theory can avoid such a constraint.

Certainly, there is a difference between discussing the letter mentioned by Wilkins and discussing *Finnegans Wake. Finnegans Wake* can help us to cast in doubt even the supposed commonsensicality of Wilkins's example. But we cannot disregard the point of view of the slave who witnessed for the first time the miracle of texts and of their interpretation. If there is something to be interpreted, the interpretation must speak of something which must be found somewhere, and in some way respected. Thus, at least for the course of my next lecture, my proposal is: let us first rank with the slave. It is the only way to become, if not the masters, at least the respectful servants of semiosis.

2

Overinterpreting texts

UMBERTO ECO

In 'Interpretation and history' I looked at a method of interpreting the world and texts based on the individuation of the relationships of sympathy that link microcosm and macrocosm to one another. Both a metaphysic and a physic of universal sympathy must stand upon a semiotics (explicit or implicit) of similarity. Michel Foucault has already dealt with the paradigm of similarity in *Les mots et les choses*, but there he was principally concerned with that threshold moment between the Renaissance and the seventeenth century in which the paradigm of similarity dissolves into the paradigm of modern science. My hypothesis is historically more comprehensive and is intended to highlight an interpretive criterion (which I call Hermetic semiosis) the survival of which can be traced through the centuries.

In order to assume that the similar can act upon the similar, the Hermetic semiosis had to decide what similarity was. But its criterion of similarity displayed an over-indulgent generality and flexibility. It included not only those phenomena that today we would list under the heading of morphological resemblance or proportional analogy, but every kind of possible substitution permitted by the rhetoric tradition, that is, contiguity, *pars pro toto*, action or actor, and so on and so forth.

I have drawn the following list of criteria for associating images or words not from a treatise on magic but from a sixteenth-century mnemonics or *ars memoriae*. The quotation is interesting because – quite apart from any Hermetic presumption – the author has identified in the context of his own culture a number of associative automatisms commonly accepted as effective.

1 By similitude, which is in turn subdivided into similitude of substance (man as a microcosmic image of the macrocosm), quality (the ten figures for the ten commandments), by metonymy and antonomasia (Atlas for astronomers or astronomy, the bear for an irascible man, the lion for pride, Cicero for rhetoric).
2 By homonymy: the animal dog for the constellation Dog.
3 By irony or contrast: the fool for the sage.
4 By sign: the spoor for the wolf, or the mirror in which Titus admired himself for Titus.
5 By a word of different pronunciation: *sanum* for *sane*.
6 By similarity of name: Arista for Aristotle.
7 By type and species: leopard for animal.
8 By pagan symbol: eagle for Jupiter.
9 By peoples: the Parthians for arrows, the Scythians for horses, the Phoenicians for the alphabet.
10 By signs of the Zodiac: the sign for the constellation.
11 By the relationship between organ and function.
12 By a common characteristic: the crow for Ethiopians.
13 By hieroglyphics: the ant for Providence.
14 And finally, pure idiolectal association, any monster for anything to be remembered.[1]

As can be seen, sometimes the two things are similar for their behaviour, sometimes for their shape, sometimes for the fact

[1] Cosma Rosselli, *Thesaurus artificiosae memoriae* (Venice, 1589).

that in a certain context they appeared together. As long as some kind of relationship can be established, the criterion does not matter. Once the mechanism of analogy has been set in motion there is no guarantee that it will stop. The image, the concept, the truth that is discovered beneath the veil of similarity, will in its turn be seen as a sign of another analogical deferral. Every time one thinks to have discovered a similarity, it will point to another similarity, in an endless progress. In a universe dominated by the logic of similarity (and cosmic sympathy) the interpreter has the right and the duty to suspect that what one believed to be the meaning of a sign is in fact the sign for a further meaning.

This makes clear another underlying principle of Hermetic semiosis. If two things are similar, the one can become the sign for the other and vice versa. Such a passage from similarity to semiosis is not automatic. This pen is similar to that one, but this does not lead us to conclude that I can use the former in order to designate the latter (except in particular cases of signification by ostension, in which, let's say, I show you this pen in order to ask you to give me the other one or some object performing the same function; but semiosis by ostension requires a previous agreement). The word *dog* is not similar to a dog. The portrait of Queen Elizabeth on a British stamp is similar (under a certain description) to a given human person who is the queen of the United Kingdom, and through the reference to her it can become the emblem for the UK. The word *pig* is neither similar to a swine nor to Noriega or Ceauscescu; nevertheless, on the grounds of a culturally established analogy between the physical habits of swine and the moral habits of dictators, I can use the word *pig* to designate one of the above-mentioned gentlemen. A semiotic analysis of such a complex notion as similarity (see my analysis in *A Theory of Semiotics*) can help us to isolate the basic flaws of the Hermetic semiosis and through it the basic flaws of many procedures of overinterpretation.

It is indisputable that human beings think (also) in terms of identity and similarity. In everyday life, however, it is a fact that we generally know how to distinguish between relevant, significant similarities on the one hand and fortuitous, illusory similarities on the other. We may see someone in the distance whose features remind us of person A, whom we know, mistake him for A, and then realize that in fact it is B, a stranger: after which, usually, we abandon our hypothesis as to the person's identity and give no further credence to the similarity, which we record as fortuitous. We do this because each of us has introjected into him or her an indisputable fact, namely, that *from a certain point of view everything bears relationships of analogy, contiguity and similarity to everything else*. One may push this to its limits and state that there is a relationship between the adverb 'while' and the noun 'crocodile' because – at least – they both appeared in the sentence that I have just uttered. But the difference between the sane interpretation and paranoiac interpretation lies in recognizing that this relationship is minimal, and not, on the contrary, deducing from this minimal relationship the maximum possible. The paranoiac is not the person who notices that 'while' and 'crocodile' curiously appear in the same context: the paranoiac is the person who begins to wonder about the mysterious motives that induced me to bring these two particular words together. The paranoiac sees beneath my example a secret, to which I allude.

In order to read both the world and texts suspiciously one must have elaborated some kind of obsessive method. Suspicion, in itself, is not pathological: both the detective and the scientist suspect on principle that some elements, evident but not apparently important, may be evidence of something else that is not evident – and on this basis they elaborate a new hypothesis to be tested. But the evidence is considered as a sign of something else only on three conditions: that it cannot be explained more economically; that it points to a single cause (or a limited class of possible causes) and not to an indeterminate number of dissimilar causes; and that it fits in with the other evidence. If at the scene of a crime I find a copy of the most widely circulated morning paper, I must first of all ask (the criterion of economy) whether it might not have belonged to the victim; if it did not, the clue would point to a million potential suspects. If, on the other hand, at the scene of the crime I find a jewel of rare form, deemed the unique example of its kind, generally known to belong to a certain individual, the clue becomes interesting; and if I then find that this individual is unable to show me his own jewel, then the two clues fit in with each other. Note, however, that at this point my conjecture is not yet proved. It merely seems reasonable, and it is reasonable because it allows me to establish some of the conditions in which it could be falsified: if, for example, the suspect were able to provide incontrovertible proof that he had given the jewel to the victim a long time before, then the presence of the jewel on the scene of the crime would no longer be an important clue.

The overestimation of the importance of clues is often born of a propensity to consider the most immediately apparent elements as significant, whereas the very fact that they are apparent should allow us to recognize that they are explicable in much more economical terms. One example of the ascription of pertinence to the wrong element provided by the theorists of scientific induction is the following: if a doctor notices that all his patients suffering from cirrhosis of the liver regularly drink either whisky and soda, cognac and soda, or gin and soda, and concludes from this that soda causes cirrhosis of the liver, he is wrong. He is wrong because he does not notice that there is another element common to the three cases, namely alcohol, and he is wrong because he ignores all the cases of teetotal patients who drink only soda and do not have cirrhosis of the liver. Now, the example seems ridiculous precisely because the doctor fixes upon what could be explained in other ways and not upon what he should have wondered about; and he does so because it is easier to notice the presence of water, which is evident, than the presence of alcohol.

Hermetic semiosis goes too far precisely in the practices of suspicious interpretation, according to *principles of facility* which appear in all the texts of this tradition. First of all, an excess of wonder leads to overestimating the importance of coincidences which are explainable in other ways. The Hermeticism of the Renaissance was looking for 'signatures', that is, visible clues revealing occult relationships. The tradition had discovered, for example, that the plant called orchis had two spheroidal bulbs, and they had seen in this a remarkable morphological analogy with the testicles. On the basis of this resemblance they proceeded to the *homologation of different relationships*: from the morphological analogy they passed to the functional analogy. The orchis could not but have magical properties with regard to the reproductive apparatus (hence it was also known as satyrion).

In actual fact, as Bacon later explained ('Parasceve ad historiam naturalem et experimentalem', in the Appendix to *Novum Organum*, 1620), the orchis has two bulbs because a new bulb is formed every year and grows beside the old one; and while the former grows, the latter withers. Thus the bulbs may demonstrate a formal analogy with the testicles, but they have a different function with respect to the fertilization process. And, as the magic relationship must be of a functional type, the analogy does not hold. The morphological phenomenon cannot be evidence of a relationship of cause and effect because it does not fit in with other data concerning causal relationships. Hermetic thought made use of a principle of *false transitivity*, by which it is assumed that if A bears a relationship x to B, and B bears a relationship y to C, then A must bear a relationship y to C. If the bulbs bear a relationship of morphological resemblance to the testicles and the testicles bear a causal relationship to the production of semen, it does not follow that the bulbs are causally connected to sexual activity.

But the belief in the magic power of the orchis was sustained by another Hermetic principle, namely the short circuit of the *post hoc, ergo ante hoc*: a consequence is assumed and interpreted as the cause of its own cause. That the orchis must bear a relationship to the testicles was proved by the fact that the former bore the name of the latter ('orchis' = 'testicle'). Of course, the etymology was the result of a false clue. Nevertheless, Hermetic thought saw in the etymology the evidence that proved the occult sympathy.

The Renaissance Hermetists believed that the *Corpus Hermeticum* had been written by a mythical Trismegistos who lived in Egypt before Moses. Isaac Casaubon proved at the beginning of the seventeenth century not only that a text which bears traces of Christian thought had to be written after Christ but also that the text of the *Corpus* did not bear any trace of Egyptian idioms. The whole of the occult tradition after Casaubon disregarded the second remark and used the first one in terms of *post hoc, ergo ante hoc*: if the *Corpus* contains ideas that were afterwards supported by the Christian thought, this meant that it was written before Christ and influenced Christianity.

I shall show in a while that we can find similar procedures in contemporary practices of textual interpretation. Our problem is, however, the following: we know that the analogy between satyrion and testicles was a wrong one because empirical tests have demonstrated that that plant cannot act upon our body. We can reasonably believe that the *Corpus Hermeticum* was not so archaic because we do not have any philological proof of the existence of its manuscripts before the end of the first millennium AD. But by what criterion do we decide that a given textual interpretation is an instance of overinterpretation? One can object that in order to define a bad interpretation one needs the criteria for defining a good interpretation.

I think, on the contrary, that we can accept a sort of Popperian principle according to which if there are no rules that help to ascertain which interpretations are the 'best' ones, there is at least a rule for ascertaining which ones are 'bad'. We cannot say if the Keplerian hypotheses are definitely the best ones but we can say that the Ptolemaic explanation of the solar system was wrong because the notions of epicycle and deferent violated certain criteria of economy or simplicity, and could not coexist with other hypotheses that proved to be reliable in order to explain phenomena that Ptolemy did not explain. Let me for the moment assume my criterion of textual economy without a previous definition of it.

Let me examine a blatant case of overinterpretation à propos secular sacred texts. Forgive me the oxymoron. As soon as a text becomes 'sacred' for a certain culture, it becomes subject to the process of suspicious reading and therefore to what is undoubtedly an excess of interpretation. It had happened, with classical allegory, in the case of the Homeric texts, and it could not but have happened in the patristic and scholastic periods with the Scriptures, as in Jewish culture with the interpretation of the Torah. But in the case of texts which are sacred, properly speaking, one cannot allow oneself too much licence, as there is usually a religious authority and tradition that claims to hold the key to its interpretation. Medieval culture, for example, did everything it could to encourage an interpretation that was infinite in terms of time but nevertheless limited in its options. If anything characterized the theory of the fourfold sense of Scripture it was that the senses of Scripture (and, for Dante, of secular poetry as well) were four in number; but senses had to be determined according to precise rules, and these senses, though hidden beneath the literal surface of the words, were not secret at all but, on the contrary – for those who know how to read the text correctly – had to be clear. And if they were not clear at first sight, it was the task of the exegetic tradition (in the case of the Bible) or the poet (for his works) to provide the key. This is what Dante does in the *Convivio* and in other writings such as the *Epistula XIII*.

This attitude toward sacred texts (in the literal sense of the term) has also been transmitted, in secularized form, to texts which have become metaphorically sacred in the course of their reception. It happened in the medieval world to Virgil; it happened in France to Rabelais; it happened to Shakespeare (under the banner of the 'Bacon–Shakespeare controversy' a legion of secret-hunters have sacked the texts of the Bard word by word, letter by letter, to find anagrams, acrostics, and other secret messages through which Francis Bacon might have made it clear that he was the true author of the 1623 Folio); and it is happening, maybe too much, to Joyce. Such being the case, Dante could hardly have been left out.

Thus we see that – starting from the second half of the nineteenth century up to now – from the early works of the Anglo-Italian author Gabriele Rossetti (father of the better-known pre-Raphaelite painter Dante Gabriel), of the French Eugène Aroux, or of the great Italian poet Giovanni Pascoli, up to René Guenon, many critics have obsessively read and re-read Dante's immense opus in order to find in it a hidden message.

Notice that Dante was the first to say that his poetry conveyed a non-literal sense, to be detected 'sotto il velame delli versi strani', beyond and beneath the literal sense. But not only did Dante explicitly assert this; he also furnished the keys for finding out non-literal senses. Nevertheless, these interpreters, whom we shall call Followers of the Veil (Adepti del Velame), identify in Dante a secret language or jargon on the basis of which every reference to erotic matters and to real people is to be interpreted as a coded invective against the Church. Here one might reasonably ask why Dante should have gone to such trouble to conceal his Ghibelline passions, given that he did nothing but issue explicit invective against the papal seat. The Followers of the Veil evoke someone who, upon being told 'Sir, you are a thief, believe me!' replies with: 'What do you mean by "believe me"? Do you perhaps wish to insinuate that I am distrustful?'

The bibliography of the Followers of the Veil is incredibly rich. And it is incredible to what extent the mainstream of Dantesque criticism ignored or disregarded it. Recently I encouraged selected young researchers to read – maybe for the first time – all those books.[2] The aim of the research was not so much to decide whether the Followers of the Veil were wrong or not (it happens that in many instances, by a felicitous case of serendipity, they were probably right), but rather to evaluate the economic value of their hypotheses.

Let us examine a concrete example in which Rossetti deals with one of the paramount obsessions of the Followers of the

---

[2] M.P. Pozzato (ed.), *L'idea deforme: Interpretazioni esoteriche di Dante* (Milan, Bompiani, 1989).

Veil.[3] According to them, Dante in his text depicts a number of symbols and liturgical practices typical of the Masonic and Rosicrucian traditions. This is an interesting question that runs into a historical–philological problem: while documents exist which attest to the rise of Rosicrucian ideas at the beginning of the seventeenth century and the appearance of the first lodges of symbolic Freemasonry at the beginning of the eighteenth century, there are none – none at least that are accepted by serious scholars – attesting to the earlier existence of these ideas and/or organizations. On the contrary, reliable documents exist which attest to how in the eighteenth and nineteenth centuries various lodges and societies of different tendencies chose rites and symbols which would demonstrate their Rosicrucian and Templar lineage. Indeed, any organization that claims its own descent from an earlier tradition chooses for its emblems those of the tradition to which it refers back (see, for example, the Italian Fascist party's choice of the lictor's fasces as a sign that they wished to consider themselves the heirs of ancient Rome). Such choices provide clear proof of the intentions of the group, but do not provide proof of any direct descent.

Rossetti sets out with the conviction that Dante was a Freemason, Templar, and member of the Fraternity of the Rosy Cross, and he therefore assumes that a Masonic–Rosicrucian symbol would be as follows: a rose with the cross inside it, under which appears a pelican that, in accordance with traditional legend, feeds its young with the flesh it tears from its own breast. Now, Rossetti's task is to prove that this symbol also appears in Dante. It is true that he runs the risk of demonstrating merely the only reasonable hypothesis, namely

---

3 Gabriele Rossetti, *La Beatrice di Dante*, ninth and final discussion, part I, art. 2 (Rome, Atanor, 1982), pp. 519–25.

that Masonic symbology was inspired by Dante, but at this point another hypothesis could be advanced: that of a third archetypal text. In this way Rossetti would kill two birds with one stone: he would be able to prove not only that the Masonic tradition is an ancient one, but also that Dante himself was inspired by this ancient tradition.

Normally one accepts the idea that if document B was produced before document C, which is analogous to the first in terms of content and style, it is correct to assume that the first influenced the production of the second but not vice versa. One could at most formulate the hypothesis of an archetypal document, A, produced before the other two, from which the two later ones both drew independently. The hypothesis of an archetypal text may be useful in order to explain analogies between two known documents that would otherwise be unaccountable: but it is necessary only if the analogies (the clues) cannot otherwise, and more economically, be explained. If we find two texts of different periods both of which mention the murder of Julius Caesar, there is no need to suppose either that the first influenced the second or that they were both influenced by an archetypal text, because here we are dealing with an event that was, and still is, reported in countless other texts.

Worse can happen, however: in order to show the excellence of C, one needs an archetypal text A on which B and C depend. Since, however, A is not to be found, then it is fideistically postulated as being in all respects identical to C. The optical effect is that C influenced B, and thus we have the *post hoc, ergo ante hoc* effect. Rossetti's tragedy is that he does not find in Dante any remarkable analogy with Masonic symbology, and having no analogies to lead him to an archetype, he does not even know what archetype to look for.

If we are to decide whether the phrase 'the rose is blue'

appears in the text of an author, it is necessary to find in the text the complete phrase 'the rose is blue'. If we find on page 1 the article 'the', on page 50 the sequence 'ros' in the body of the lexeme 'rosary' and so on, we have proved nothing, because it is obvious that, given the limited number of letters in the alphabet that a text combines, with such a method we could find any statement we wish in any text whatsoever.

Rossetti is surprised that in Dante we find references to the cross, the rose, and the pelican. The reasons for the appearance of these words are self-evident. In a poem that speaks of the mysteries of the Christian religion it is not surprising that sooner or later the symbol of the Passion should appear. On the basis of an ancient symbolic tradition, the pelican became the symbol of Christ very early on in the Christian tradition (and medieval bestiaries and religious poetry are full of references to this symbol). As regards the rose, because of its complex symmetry, its softness, the variety of its colours, and the fact that it flowers in spring, it appears in nearly all mystical traditions as a symbol, metaphor, allegory, or simile for freshness, youth, feminine grace, and beauty in general. For all these reasons, what Rossetti himself calls the 'fresh, sweet-smelling rose' appears as a symbol of feminine beauty in another poet of the thirteenth century, Ciullo d'Alcamo, and as an erotic symbol both in Apuleius and in a text which Dante knew well, the *Roman de la Rose* (which in its turn intention-ally makes use of pagan symbology). Thus, when Dante has to represent the supernatural glory of the Church triumphant in terms of splendour, love, and beauty, he resorts to the figure of the spotless rose (*Paradiso*, XXXI). Incidentally, since the Church triumphant is the bride of Christ as a direct result of the Passion, Dante cannot avoid observing that 'Christ made (the Church) his bride by his blood'; and this allusion to blood is the only case among the texts presented by Rossetti in which, by inference, the rose can be seen in reference (conceptual, but not iconographic) to the cross. '*Rosa*' appears in the *Divine Comedy* eight times in the singular and three in the plural. '*Croce*' appears seventeen times. But they never appear together.

Rossetti, however, wants the pelican as well. He finds it, on its own, in *Paradiso* XXXVI (its only appearance in the poem), clearly in connection with the cross, for the pelican is the symbol of sacrifice. Unfortunately, the rose is not there. So Rossetti goes in search of other pelicans. He finds a pelican in Cecco d'Ascoli (another author over whom the Followers of the Veil have racked their brains for the very reason that the text of *L'Acerba* is intentionally obscure), and Cecco's pelican appears in the usual context of the Passion, Moreover, a pelican in Cecco is not a pelican in Dante, even though Rossetti tries to blur such a minor difference by confusing the footnotes. Rossetti believes he has found another pelican in that incipit of *Paradiso* XXIII, where we read of the fowl that, waiting impatiently for the dawn, sits alert among the beloved fronds on a leafy branch watching for the sunrise so as to go and find food for its young. Now, this bird, graceful indeed, searches for food precisely because it is not a pelican, otherwise it would not need to go hunting, as it could easily feed its young with flesh torn from its own breast. Second, it appears as a simile for Beatrice, and it would have been poetic suicide had Dante represented his beloved by the awkward features of a billed pelican. Rossetti, in his desperate and rather pathetic fowling, could find in the divine poem seven fowls and eleven birds and ascribe them all to the pelican family: but he would find them all far from the rose.

Examples of this kind abound in Rossetti's work. I will cite only one other, which appears in Canto II, which is generally considered one of the most philosophic and doctrinal of the whole *Paradiso*. This canto exploits fully a device which is a basic element in the whole of the third book: the divine mysteries, otherwise inexpressible, are represented in terms of light – in full accord with theological and mystic tradition. Consequently, even the most difficult philosophical concepts must be expressed with optical examples. It should be noted here that Dante was led to this choice by all the literature of the theology and physics of his time: Arabic treatises dealing with optics had reached the Western world only a few decades earlier; Robert Grosseteste had explained cosmogonic phenomena in terms of light energy; in the theological field Bonaventura had debated the difference between '*lux*', '*lumen*', and '*color*'; the *Roman de la Rose* had celebrated the magic of mirrors and had described phenomena of the reflection, refraction, and magnification of images; Roger Bacon had claimed for optics the dignity of a major and fundamental science, reproaching the Parisians for not considering it enough, while the English were investigating its principles. It is obvious that, having used the similes of a diamond struck by the sun, of a gem, and of a mass of water penetrated by a ray of light to describe a number of astronomical phenomena, Dante, faced with having to explain the different brightnesses of the fixed stars, should have recourse to an optical explanation and propose the example of three mirrors which, placed at different distances, reflect the rays of a single source of light.

For Rossetti, however, in this canto Dante would be 'whimsical' if we did not take into account that three lights arranged in a triangle – three sources of light, note, which is not the same as three mirrors reflecting the light of another source – appear in Masonic ritual.[4] Even if we accept the principle of *post hoc, ergo ante hoc*, however, this hypothesis would at most explain why Dante (knowing Masonic rituals of a later date!)

[4] Ibid, p. 406.

chose the image of three sources of light, but it does not explain the rest of the canto.

Thomas Kuhn observes that to be accepted as a paradigm, a theory must seem better than the other theories in the lists but need not necessarily explain all the facts with which it is concerned. Let me add, however, that neither must it explain less than previous theories. If we accept that here Dante is speaking in terms of medieval optics, we may also understand why in verses 89–90 he speaks of the colour that 'turns through glass – which hides lead behind it'. If, on the other hand, Dante is speaking of Masonic lights, the other lights of the canto remain obscure.

Let me now consider a case where the rightness of the interpretation is undecidable, but where it is assuredly difficult to assert that it is wrong. It can happen that certain more or less esoteric interpretive practices recall those of certain deconstructionist critics. But in the shrewdest representatives of this school the hermeneutic game does not exclude interpretive rules.

Here is how one of the leaders of the Yale deconstructionists, Geoffrey Hartman, examines some lines from Wordsworth's 'Lucy' poems, in which the poet speaks explicitly of the death of a girl:

> I had no human *fears*:
> She seemed a thing that could not feel
> The touch of earthly *years*.
> No motion has she now, no force;
> She neither *hears* nor sees,
> Rolled round in earth's *diurnal course*
> With rocks and stones and *trees*.

Hartman sees here a series of funereal motifs under the surface of the text.

Others even show Wordsworth's language penetrated by an inappropriate subliminal punning. So 'diurnal' (line 6) divides into 'die' and 'urn', and 'course' may recall the older pronunciation of 'corpse'. Yet these condensations are troublesome rather than expressive; the power of the second stanza resides predominantly in the euphemistic displacement of the word 'grave' by an image of gravitation ('Rolled round in earth's diurnal course'). And though there is no agreement on the tone of this stanza, it is clear that a subvocal word is uttered without being written out. It is a word that rhymes with 'fears' and 'years' and 'hears', but which is closed off by the very last syllable of the poem: 'trees'. Read 'tears' and the animating, cosmic metaphor comes alive, the poet's lament echoes through nature as in pastoral elegy. 'Tears', however, must give way to what is written, to a dull yet definitive sound, the anagram 'trees'.[5]

It must be noted that, while 'die', 'urn', 'corpse', and 'tears' can be in some way suggested by other terms that appear in the text (namely, 'diurnal', 'course', 'fears', 'years', and 'hears'), 'grave' is, on the contrary, suggested by a 'gravitation' which does not appear in the text but is produced by a paraphrastic decision of the reader. Furthermore, 'tears' is not the anagram of 'trees'. If we want to prove that a visible text A is the anagram of a hidden text B, we must show that all the letters of A, duly reorganized, produce B. If we start to discard some letters, the game is no longer valid. *Top* is an anagram of *pot*, but not of *port*. There is, thus, a constant oscillation (I do not know how acceptable) between the phonic similarity of terms *in praesentia* and the phonic similarity of terms *in absentia*. In spite of this, Hartman's reading sounds, if not fully convincing, at least charming.

Hartman is certainly not suggesting here that Wordsworth actually wished to produce these associations – such searching

5   Geoffrey H. Hartman, *Easy Pieces* (New York, Columbia University Press, 1985), pp. 149–50.

after the author's intentions would not fit Hartman's critical principles. He simply wishes to say that it is legitimate for a sensitive reader to find what he finds in the text, because these associations are, at least potentially, evoked by the text, and because the poet might (perhaps unconsciously) have created some 'harmonics' to the main theme. If it is not the author, let us say it is the language which has created this echo effect. As far as Wordsworth is concerned, though on the one hand nothing proves that the text suggests neither tomb nor tears, on the other hand nothing excludes it. The tomb and the tears evoked belong to the same semantic field as the lexemes *in praesentia*. Hartman's reading does not contradict other explicit aspects of the text. One may judge his interpretation too generous, but not economically absurd. The evidence may be weak, but it does fit in.

In theory, one can always invent a system that renders otherwise unconnected clues plausible. But in the case of texts there is at least a proof depending on the isolation of the relevant semantic isotopy. Greimas defines 'isotopy' as 'a complex of manifold semantic categories making possible the uniform reading of a story'.[6] The most flashing and maybe the most sophomoric example of contradictory readings due to the possible isolation of different textual isotopies is the following: two fellows talk during a party and the first praises the food, the service, the generosity of the hosts, the beauty of the female guests, and, finally, the excellence of the 'toilettes'; the second replies that he has not yet been there. This is a joke, and we laugh about the second fellow, because he interprets the French term 'toilette', which is polysemic, in the sense of sanitary facilities and not of garments and fashion. He is wrong because the whole of the discourse of the first fellow was

6   A.J. Greimas, *Du sens* (Paris, Seuil, 1979), p. 88.

concerning a social event and not a question of plumbing. The first movement toward the recognition of a semantic isotopy is a conjecture about the topic of a given discourse: once this conjecture has been attempted, the recognition of a possible constant semantic isotopy is the textual proof of the 'aboutness' of the discourse in question.[7] If the second fellow had attempted to infer that the first one was speaking of the various aspects of a social event, he would have been able to decide that the lexeme 'toilettes' had to be interpreted accordingly.

Deciding what is being talked about is, of course, a kind of interpretive bet. But the contexts allow us to make this bet less uncertain than a bet on the red or the black of a roulette wheel. The funereal interpretation of Hartman has the advantage of betting on a constant isotopy. Bets on the isotopy are certainly a good interpretive criterion, but only as long as the isotopies are not too generic. This is a principle which is valid also for metaphors. A metaphor exists when we substitute a vehicle for the tenor on the basis of one or more semantic traits common to both the linguistic terms: but if Achilles is a lion because both are courageous and fierce, we would be inclined to reject the metaphor 'Achilles is a duck' if it were justified on the basis of the principle that both are bipeds. Few others are as courageous as Achilles and the lion, whereas far too many others are bipeds like Achilles and the duck. A similarity or an analogy, whatever its epistemological status, is important if it is exceptional, at least under a certain description. An analogy between Achilles and a clock based on the fact that both are physical objects is of no interest whatsoever.

The classical debate aimed at finding in a text either what its author intended to say, or what the text said independently of

---

[7] Cf. Umberto Eco, *The Role of the Reader* (Bloomington, Indiana University Press, 1979), p. 195.

the intentions of its author. Only after accepting the second horn of the dilemma can one ask if what is found is what the text says by virtue of its textual coherence and of an original underlying signification system, or what the addressees found in it by virtue of their own systems of expectations.

It is clear that I am trying to keep a dialectical link between *intentio operis* and *intentio lectoris*. The problem is that, if one perhaps knows what is meant by 'intention of the reader', it seems more difficult to define abstractly what is meant by 'intention of the text'. The text's intention is not displayed by the textual surface. Or, if it is displayed, it is so in the sense of the purloined letter. One has to decide to 'see' it. Thus it is possible to speak of the text's intention only as the result of a conjecture on the part of the reader. The initiative of the reader basically consists in making a conjecture about the text's intention.

A text is a device conceived in order to produce its model reader. I repeat that this reader is not the one who makes the 'only right' conjecture. A text can foresee a model reader entitled to try infinite conjectures. The empirical reader is only an actor who makes conjectures about the kind of model reader postulated by the text. Since the intention of the text is basically to produce a model reader able to make conjectures about it, the initiative of the model reader consists in figuring out a model author that is not the empirical one and that, in the end, coincides with the intention of the text. Thus, more than a parameter to use in order to validate the interpretation, the text is an object that the interpretation builds up in the course of the circular effort of validating itself on the basis of what it makes up as its result. I am not ashamed to admit that I am so defining the old and still valid 'hermeneutic circle'.

To recognize the *intentio operis* is to recognize a semiotic strategy. Sometimes the semiotic strategy is detectable on the grounds of established stylistic conventions. If a story starts with 'Once upon a time', there is a good probability that it is a fairy tale and that the evoked and postulated model reader is a child (or an adult eager to react in a childish mood). Naturally, I can witness a case of irony, and as a matter of fact the following text should be read in a more sophisticated way. But even though I can discover by the further course of the text that this is the case, it has been indispensable to recognize that the text pretended to start as a fairy tale.

How to prove a conjecture about the *intentio operis*? The only way is to check it upon the text as a coherent whole. This idea, too, is an old one and comes from Augustine (*De doctrina christiana*): any interpretation given of a certain portion of a text can be accepted if it is confirmed by, and must be rejected if it is challenged by, another portion of the same text. In this sense the internal textual coherence controls the otherwise uncontrollable drives of the reader. Borges (à propos his character Pierre Ménard) suggested that it would be exciting to read the *Imitation of Christ* as if it were written by Céline.[8] The game is amusing and could be intellectually fruitful. I tried; I discovered sentences that could have been written by Céline ('Grace loves low things and is not disgusted by thorny ones, and likes filthy clothes'). But this kind of reading offers a suitable 'grid' for very few sentences of the *Imitatio*. All the rest, most of the book, resists this reading. If on the contrary I read the book according to the Christian medieval encyclopedia, it appears textually coherent in each of its parts.

I realize that, in this dialectics between the intention of the reader and the intention of the text, the intention of the empirical author has been totally disregarded. Are we entitled to ask what was the 'real' intention of Wordsworth when

---

[8] Jorge Luis Borges, *Ficciónes* (Buenos Aires, Sur, 1944).

writing his 'Lucy' poems? My idea of textual interpretation as the discovery of a strategy intended to produce a model reader, conceived as the ideal counterpart of a model author (which appears only as a textual strategy), makes the notion of an empirical author's intention radically useless. We have to respect the text, not the author as person so-and-so. Nevertheless, it can look rather crude to eliminate the poor author as something irrelevant for the story of an interpretation. There are, in the process of communication, cases in which an inference about the intention of the speaker is absolutely important, as this always happens in everyday communication. An anonymous letter reading 'I am happy' can refer to an infinite range of possible subjects of the utterance, that is, to the entire class of persons who believe themselves not to be sad; but if I, in this precise moment, utter the sentence 'I am happy' it is absolutely certain that my intention was to say that that happy one is me and not someone else, and you are invited to make such an assumption, for the sake of the felicity of our interaction. Can we (likewise) take into account cases of interpretation of written texts to which the empirical author, still alive, reacts by saying 'No, I did not mean that'? This will be the topic of my next lecture.

3

Between author and text

UMBERTO ECO

I ended 'Overinterpreting texts' with a dramatic question: can we still be concerned with the empirical author of a text? When I speak with a friend I am interested in detecting the intention of the speaker, and when I receive a letter from a friend I am interested in realizing what the writer wanted to say. In this sense I feel perplexed when I read the *jeu de massacre* performed by Derrida upon a text signed by John Searle.[1] Or, rather, I take it only as a splendid exercise in philosophical paradoxes, without forgetting that Zeno, when demonstrating the impossibility of movement, was nevertheless aware that for doing that he had at least to move both his tongue and his lips. There is a case, however, where I feel sympathetic with many reader-oriented theories. When a text is put in the bottle – and this happens not only with poetry or narrative but also with *The Critique of Pure Reason* – that is, when a text is produced not for a single addressee but for a community of readers – the author knows that he or she will be interpreted not according to his or her intentions but according to a complex strategy of interactions which also involves the readers, along with their competence in language as a social treasury. I mean by social treasury not only a given language as a set of grammatical rules,

[1] Jaques Derrida, 'Limited Inc.', *Glyph*, 2 (1977), 162–254.

but also the whole encyclopedia that the performances of that
language have implemented, namely, the cultural conventions
that that language has produced and the very history of the
previous interpretations of many texts, comprehending the
text that the reader is in the course of reading.

The act of reading must evidently take into account all these elements, even though it is improbable that a single reader can master all of them. Thus every act of reading is a difficult transaction between the competence of the reader (the reader's world knowledge) and the kind of competence that a given text postulates in order to be read in an economic way. In his *Criticism in the Wilderness* Hartman made a subtle analysis of Wordsworth's poem 'I wander lonely as a cloud.'[2] I remember that in 1985, during a debate at Northwestern University I said to Hartman that he was a 'moderate' deconstructionist because he refrained from reading the line

'A poet could not but be gay'

as a contemporary reader would do if the line were found in *Playboy*. In other words, a sensitive and responsible reader is not obliged to speculate about what happened in the head of Wordsworth when writing that verse, but has the duty to take into account the state of the lexical system at the time of Wordsworth. At that time 'gay' had no sexual connotation, and to acknowledge this point means to interact with a cultural and social treasury.

In my *The Role of the Reader* I stressed the difference between interpreting and using a text. I can certainly use Wordsworth's text for parody, for showing how a text can be read in relation to different cultural frameworks, or for strictly personal ends (I can read a text to get inspiration for my own

---

[2] Geoffrey Hartman, *Criticism in the Wilderness*, (New Haven, Yale University Press, 1980) p. 28.

musing); but if I want to *interpret* Wordsworth's text I must
respect his cultural and linguistic background.

What happens if I find the text of Wordsworth in a bottle
and I do not know when it was written or by whom? I shall
look, after having met the word 'gay' to see if the further course
of the text supports a sexual interpretation, so to encourage me
to believe that 'gay' also conveyed connotations of homosexu-
ality. If so, and if clearly or at least persuasively so, I can try the
hypothesis that that text was not written by a Romantic poet
but by a contemporary writer – who was perhaps imitating the
style of a romantic poet. In the course of such a complex
interaction between my knowledge and the knowledge I
impute to the unknown author, I am not speculating about the
author's intentions but about the text's intention, or about the
intention of that Model Author that I am able to recognize in
terms of textual strategy.

When Lorenzo Valla demonstrated that the *Constitutum
Constantini* was a forgery he was probably influenced by his
personal prejudice that the emperor Constantine never wanted
to give the temporal power to the Pope, but in writing his
philological analysis he was not concerned with the interpretation of Constantine's intentions. He simply showed that the
use of certain linguistic expressions was implausible at the
beginning of the fourth century. The Model Author of the
alleged Donation could not have been a Roman writer of that
period. Recently one of my students, Mauro Ferraresi, suggested that between the empirical author and the Model
Author (which is nothing else than an explicit textual strategy)
there is a third, rather ghostly, figure that he christened
Liminal Author, or the Author on the Threshold – the
threshold between the intention of a given human being and
the linguistic intention displayed by a textual strategy.

Returning to Hartman's analysis of Wordsworth's 'Lucy'

poems (quoted in my second lecture), the intention of Wordsworth's text was certainly – it would be difficult to doubt it – to suggest by the use of the rhyme a strong relationship between 'fears' and 'years', 'force' and 'course'. But are we sure that Mr Wordsworth in person wanted to evoke the association, introduced by the reader Hartman, between 'trees' and 'tears', and between an absent 'gravitation' and an absent 'grave'? Without being obliged to organize a séance and to press his or her fingers upon a jumping table, the reader can make the following conjecture: if a normal English-speaking human being is seduced by the semantic relationships between words *in praesentia* and words *in absentia*, why should not one suspect that even Wordsworth was unconsciously seduced by these possible echo-effects? I, the reader, do not attribute an explicit intention to Mr Wordsworth; I only suspect that on the threshold situation where Mr Wordsworth was no longer an empirical person and not yet a mere text, he obliged the words (or the words obliged him) to set up a possible series of associations.

Until which point can the reader give credit to such a ghostly image of the Liminal Author? One of the most beautiful and famous poems of Italian Romanticism is Leopardi's 'A Silvia'. It is a love song for a girl, Silvia, and it begins with the name 'Silvia':

> Silvia rimembri ancora
> quel tempo della tua vita mortale
> quando beltà splendea
> negli occhi tuoi ridenti e fuggitivi
> e tu lieta e pensosa il limitare
> di gioventù salivi?

(Silvia are you still remembering that time of your mortal life when beauty was radiating in your smiling fugitive eyes, and you, gay and pensive, were ascending the threshold of your youth?)

Do not ask me for which unconscious reasons I decided to use, for my rough translation, such words as 'threshold', 'mortal', and 'gay', which reproduce other key words of the present lecture. The interesting point is that this first strophe of the poem begins with *Silvia* and ends with *salivi*, and *salivi* is a perfect anagram of *Silvia*. This is a case in which I am obliged to look neither for the intentions of the empirical author nor for the unconscious reactions of the Liminal one. The text is there, the anagram is there, and, moreover, legions of critics have stressed the overwhelming presence of the vowel 'i' in this strophe.

We can obviously do more: we can, as I did, start looking for other anagrams of 'Silvia' in the rest of the poem. I tell you that you can find a lot of pseudo-anagrams. I say 'pseudo' because in Italian the only reliable anagram of 'Silvia' is just 'salivi'. But there can be hidden, imperfect anagrams. For instance:

> e tu SoLeVI (...)
> mIraVA IL ciel Sereno (...)
> Le VIe DorAte (...)
> queL ch'Io SentIVA in seno (...)
> che penSIeri soAVI (...)
> LA VIta umana (...)
> doLer dI mIA SVentura (...)
> moStrAVI dI Lontano.

It is possible that the Liminal Author was obsessed by the sweet sound of the beloved name. It is reasonable that the reader has the right to enjoy all these echo effects that the text qua text provides him or her. But at this point the act of reading becomes a *terrain vague* where interpretation and use inextricably merge together. The criterion of economy becomes rather weak. I think that a poet can be obsessed by a name, beyond his empirical intentions, and to explore this issue farther I turned to Petrarch who, as is universally known, was in love with a lady called Laura. It goes without saying that I found many pseudo-anagrams of Laura in Petrarch's poems. But, since I am also a very sceptical semiotician, I did something very reprehensible. I went looking for Silvia in Petrarch and for Laura in Leopardi. And I got some interesting results – even though, I admit, quantitatively less convincing.

I believe that 'Silvia' as a poem is playing upon those six letters with irrefutable evidence, but I also know that the Italian alphabet has only twenty-one letters and that there are many chances of meeting pseudo-anagrams of Silvia even in the text of the Italian Constitution. It is economical to suspect that Leopardi was obsessed by the sound of the name of Silvia, while it is less economical to do what years ago a student of mine did: look at the whole of Leopardi's poems in order to find improbable acrostics of the word 'melancholy'. It is not impossible to find them, provided you decide that the letters forming the acrostic have not to be the first of a verse and can be found by jumping here and there through the text. But this kind of grasshopper-criticism does not explain why Leopardi had to invent such a Hellenistic or early medieval device, when the whole of his poetry tells at each verse, literally and beautifully, how melancholic he was. I think it is not economical to think that he wasted his precious time with secret messages when he was so poetically committed to making his mood poignantly clear by other linguistic means. It is not economical to suspect that Leopardi acted as a character of John Le Carré when he could say what he said in a better way. I am not asserting that it is fruitless to look for concealed messages in a poetic work: I am saying that, while it is fruitful for De laudibus sanctae crucis of Raban Maur, it is preposterous for Leopardi.

There is, however, a case in which it can be interesting to

resort to the intention of the empirical author. There are cases in which the author is still living, the critics have given their interpretations of his text, and it can then be interesting to ask the author how much and to what an extent he, as an empirical person, was aware of the manifold interpretations his text supported. At this point the response of the author must not be used in order to validate the interpretations of his text, but to show the discrepancies between the author's intention and the intention of the text. The aim of the experiment is not a critical one, but, rather, a theoretical one.

There can be, finally, a case in which the author is also a textual theorist. In this case it would be possible to get from him two different sorts of reaction. In certain cases he can say, 'No, I did not mean this, but I must agree that the text says it, and I thank the reader that made me aware of it.' Or, 'Independently of the fact that I did not mean this, I think that a reasonable reader should not accept such an interpretation, because it sounds uneconomical.'

Such a procedure is a risky one, and I would not use it in an interpretive essay. I want to use it as a laboratory experiment, only today, sitting among the happy few. Please do not tell anyone about what happens today: we are irresponsibly playing, like atomic scientists trying dangerous scenarios and unmentionable war games. Thus I am here today, guinea-pig and scientist at the same time, to tell you of some reactions I had, as the author of two novels, when facing some interpretations of them.

A typical case where the author must surrender in face of the reader is the one I told about in my *Postscript on the Name of the Rose*.[3] As I read the reviews of the novel, I felt a thrill of

---

[3] Umberto Eco, *Postscript on the Name of the Rose* (New York, Harcourt Brace, 1984). The British edition is *Reflections on the Name of the Rose* (London, Secker & Warburg, 1985).

satisfaction when I found a critic who quoted a remark of William's made at the end of the trial: 'What terrifies you most in purity?', asks Adso. And William answers, 'Haste.'[4] I loved, and still love, these two lines very much. But then one of my readers pointed out to me that on the same page, Bernard Gui, threatening the cellarer with torture, says, 'Justice is not inspired by haste, as the Pseudo Apostles believe, and the justice of God has centuries at its disposal.' And the reader rightly asked me what connection I had meant to establish between the haste feared by William and the absence of haste extolled by Bernard. I was unable to answer. As a matter of fact the exchange between Adso and William does not exist in the manuscript. I added this brief dialogue in the galleys, for reasons of concinnity: I needed to insert another scansion before giving Bernard the floor again. And I completely forgot that, a little later, Bernard speaks of haste. Bernard's speech uses a stereotyped expression, the sort of thing we would expect from a judge, a commonplace on the order of 'All are equal before the law.' Alas, when juxtaposed with the haste mentioned by William, the haste mentioned by Bernard literally creates an effect of sense; and the reader is justified in wondering if the two men are saying the same thing, or if the loathing of haste expressed by William is not imperceptibly different from the loathing of haste expressed by Bernard. The text is there, and it produces its own effects. Whether I wanted it this way or not, we are now faced with a question, an ambiguous provocation; and I myself feel embarrassment in interpreting this conflict, though I realize a meaning lurks there (perhaps many meanings do).

Now, let me tell of an opposite case. Helena Costiucovich before translating into Russian (masterfully) *The Name of the*

4 Ibid., p. 85.

Rose, wrote a long essay on it.[5] At a certain point she remarks that there exists a book by Emile Henroit (*La rose de Bratislava*, 1946) in which can be found the hunting of a mysterious manuscript and a final fire in a library. The story takes place in Prague, and at the beginning of my novel I mention Prague. Moreover, one of my librarians is named Berengar, and one of the librarians of Henroit was named Berngard Marre. It is perfectly useless to say that, as an empirical author, I had never read Henroit's novel and that I did not know that it existed. I have read interpretations in which my critics found out sources of which I was fully aware, and I was very happy that they so cunningly discovered what I so cunningly concealed in order to lead them to find it (for instance, the model of the couple Serenus Zeitblom and Adrian in Thomas Mann's *Doktor Faustus* for the narrative relationship of Adso and William). I have read of sources totally unknown to me, and I was delighted that somebody believed that I was eruditely quoting them. (Recently a young medievalist told me that a blind librarian was mentioned by Cassiodorus.) I have read critical analyses in which the interpreter discovered influences of which I was unaware when writing, but I certainly had read those books in my youth and I understood that I was unconsciously influenced by them. (My friend Giorgio Celli said that among my remote readings there should have been the novels of Dmitri Mereskovskij, and I recognized that he was right.)

As an uncommitted reader of *The Name of the Rose*, I think that the argument of Helena Costiucovich does not prove anything interesting. The search for a mysterious manuscript and a fire in a library are very common literary *topoi* and I could

---

5   Helena Costiucovich, 'Umberto Eco. Imja Roso', *Sovriemiennaja hodoziest-viennaja litieratura za rubiezom*, 5 (1982), 101ff.

quote many other books which use them. Prague was mentioned at the beginning of the story, but if instead of Prague I had mentioned Budapest it would have been the same. Prague does not play a crucial role in my story. By the way, when the novel was translated in some eastern countries (long before perestroika), some translators called me and said that it was difficult to mention, just at the opening of the book, the Russian invasion of Czechoslovakia. I answered that I did not approve any change of my text and that if there was some censure the responsibility was on the publisher. Then, as a joke, I added, 'I put Prague at the beginning because it is one among my magic cities. But I also like Dublin. Put Dublin instead of Prague. It does not make any difference.' They reacted, 'But Dublin was not invaded by Russians!' I answered, 'It is not my fault.'

Finally, Berengar and Berngard can be a coincidence. In any case the Model Reader can agree that four coincidences (manuscript, fire, Prague, and Berengar) are interesting, and as an empirical author I have no right to react. All right, to put a good face on this accident, I formally acknowledge that my text had the intention of paying homage to Emile Henriot. Helena Costiucovich wrote something more to prove the analogy between me and Henriot. She said that in Henriot's novel the coveted manuscript was the original copy of the *Memoirs* of Casanova. It happens that in my novel there is a minor character called Hugh of Newcastle (and in the Italian version, Ugo di Novocastro). The conclusion of Costiucovich is that 'only by passing from one name to another is it possible to conceive of the name of the rose'. As an empirical author I could say that Hugh of Newcastle is not an invention of mine but an historical figure, mentioned in the medieval sources I used; the episode of the meeting between the Franciscan legation and the Papal representatives literally quotes a medieval chronicle of the fourteenth century. But the reader does not have to know that, and my reaction cannot be taken into account. As an uncommitted reader, however, I think I have the right to state my opinion. First of all, Newcastle is not a translation of Casanova, which should be translated as Newhouse, and a castle is not a house (besides, in Italian, or in Latin, Novocastro means New City or New Encampment). Thus Newcastle suggests Casanova in the same way it could suggest Newton. But there are other elements that can textually prove that the hypothesis of Costiucovich is uneconomical. First of all, Hugh of Newcastle shows up in the novel playing a very marginal role and having nothing to do with the library. If the text wanted to suggest a pertinent relationship between Hugh and the library (as well as between him and the manuscript) it should have said something more. But the text does not say a word about that. Second, Casanova was – at least in light of a common shared encyclopedical knowledge – a professional lover and a rake, and there is nothing in the novel which casts in doubt the virtue of Hugh. Third, there is no evident connection between a manuscript of Casanova and a manu-script of Aristotle, and there is nothing in the novel which alludes to sexual incontinence as a value to be pursued. To look for the Casanova connection does not lead anywhere. Jeanne d'Arc was born in Domrémy; this word suggests the first three musical notes (do, re, mi). Molly Bloom was in love with a tenor, Blazes Boylan; blaze can evoke the stake of Jeanne, but the hypothesis that Molly Bloom is an allegory of Jeanne d'Arc does not help to find something interesting in *Ulysses* (even though one day or another there will be a Joycean critic eager to try even this key). Obviously, I am ready to change my mind if some other interpreter demonstrates that the Casanova connection can lead to some interesting interpretive path, but for the moment – as a model Reader of my own novel – I feel entitled to say that such a hypothesis is scarcely rewarding.

Once during a debate a reader asked me what I meant by the sentence 'the supreme happiness lies in having what you have'. I felt disconcerted and I swore that I had never written the sentence. I was sure of it, and for many reasons: first, I do not think that happiness lies in having what one has, and not even Snoopy would subscribe to such a triviality. Secondly, it is improbable that a medieval character would suppose that happiness lies in having what he actually has, since happiness for the medieval mind was a future state to be reached through present suffering. Thus I repeated that I had never written that line, and my interlocutor looked at me as at an author unable to recognize what he had written.

Later I came across that quotation. It appears during the description of the erotic ecstasy of Adso in the kitchen. This episode, as the dullest of my readers can easily guess, is entirely made up of quotations from the Song of Songs and from medieval mystics. In any case, even though the reader does not find out the sources, he or she can guess that these papers depict the feelings of a young man after his first (and probably last) sexual experience. If one re-reads the line in its context (I mean the context of my text, not necessarily the context of its medieval sources), one finds that the line reads: 'O Lord, when the soul is transported, the only virtue lies in having what you see, the supreme happiness is having what you have.' Thus, happiness lies in having what you have, but not in general and in every moment of your life, but only in the moment of the ecstatic vision. This is a case in which it is unnecessary to know the intention of the empirical author: the intention of the text is blatant and, if English words have a conventional meaning, the text does not say what that reader – obeying some idiosyncratic drives – believed he or she had read. Between the unattainable intention of the author and the arguable intention of the reader there is the transparent intention of the text, which disproves an untenable interpretation.

An author who has entitled his book *The Name of the Rose* must be ready to face manifold interpretations of his title. As an empirical author I wrote that I chose that title in order to set the reader free: 'the rose is a figure so rich in meanings that by now it hasn't any meaning: Dante's mystic rose, and go lovely rose, the War of the Roses, rose thou art sick, too many rings around Rosie, a rose by any other name, a rose is a rose is a rose is a rose, the Rosicrucians'.[6] Moreover someone has discovered that some early manuscripts of *De contemptu mundi* of Bernard de Morlaix, from which I borrowed the hexameter 'stat rosa pristina nomine, nomina nuda tenemus,' read 'stat Roma pristina nomine' – which after all is more coherent with the rest of the poem, which speaks of the lost Babylonia. Thus the title of my novel, had I come across another version of Morlaix's poem, could have been *The Name of Rome* (thus acquiring fascist overtones). But the text reads *The Name of the Rose* and I understand now how difficult it was to stop the infinite series of connotations that word elicits. Probably I wanted to open the possible readings so much as to make each of them irrelevant, and as a result I have produced an inexorable series of interpretations. But the text is there, and the empirical author has to remain silent.

There are, however, once again, cases in which the empirical author has the right to react as a Model Reader. I have enjoyed the beautiful book by Robert F. Fleissner, *A Rose by Any Other Name: A Survey of Literary Flora from Shakespeare to Eco*, and I hope that Shakespeare would have been proud to find his name associated with mine.[7] Among the various connections that Fleissner finds between my rose and all the other roses of world literature there is an interesting passage: Fleissner wants to show 'how Eco's rose derived from Doyle's *Adventure of the*

6 *Reflections*, p. 3.
7 Robert F. Fleissner, *A Rose by Any Other Name: A Survey of Literary Flora from Shakespeare to Eco* (West Cornwall, Locust Hill Press, 1989).

Naval Treaty, which, in turn, owed much to Cuff's admiration of this flower in *The Moonstone*.[8] I am positively a Wilkie Collins' addict but I do not remember (and certainly I did not when writing my novel) Cuff's floral passion. I believe I have read the complete works of Arthur Conan Doyle, but I must confess that I do not remember having read *The Adventure of the Naval Treaty*. It does not matter: in my novel there are so many explicit references to Sherlock Holmes that my text can support this connection.

But in spite of my open-mindedness, I find an instance of overinterpretation when Fleissner, trying to demonstrate how much my William 'echoes' Holmes's admiration for roses, quotes this passage from my book:

'Frangula,' William said suddenly, bending over to observe a plant that, on that winter day, he recognized from the bare bush. 'A good infusion is made from the bark.'

It is curious that Fleissner stops his quotation exactly after 'bark'. My text continues, and after a comma reads: 'for haemorrhoids'. Honestly, I think that the Model Reader is not invited to take frangula as an allusion to the rose – otherwise every plant could stand for a rose, like every bird, for Rossetti, stands for a pelican.

How can, however, the empirical author disprove certain free semantic associations that the words he used in some way authorize? I was delighted by the allegorical meanings that one of the contributors to *Naming the Rose* found in such names as Umberto da Romans and Nicholas of Morimondo.[9] As for Umberto da Romans, he was a historical figure who actually wrote sermons for women. I realize that a reader can be

---

8 Ibid., p. 139.
9 M. Thomas Inge (ed.), *Naming the Rose* (Jackson, Miss., University of Mississippi Press, 1988).

tempted to think of an Umberto (Eco) who writes a 'roman', but even if the author invented such a sophormoric pun it would not add anything to the understanding of the novel. More interesting is the case of Nicholas of Morimondo; my interpreter remarked that the monk who utters at the end 'The library is on fire!' thus acknowledging the fall of the abbey as a microcosm, bears a name which suggests 'death of the world'.

As a matter of fact, I christened Nicholas from the name of the well-known abbey of Morimondo, in Italy, founded in 1136 by Cistercians coming from Morimond (Haute-Marne). When I christened Nicholas, I did not know as yet that he had to pronounce his fatal statement. In any case, for a native Italian speaker living only a few miles from Morimondo, this name evokes neither death nor world. Finally, I am not sure that Morimond comes from the verb 'mori' and the noun 'mundus' (maybe 'mond' comes from a German root and means 'moon'). It can happen that a non-Italian reader with a certain knowledge of Latin or Italian smells a semantic association with the death of a world. I was not responsible for this allusion. But what does 'I' mean? My conscious personality? My id? The play of language (of *la langue*) that was taking place in my mind when I was writing? The text is there. Rather, we can ask whether that association makes sense. Certainly not as far as the understanding of the course of narrative events is concerned, but perhaps for alerting – so to speak – the reader that the action takes place in a culture where *nomina sunt numina*, or instruments of the divine revelation.

I called one of the main characters of my *Foucault's Pendulum* Casaubon and I was thinking of Isaac Casaubon, who demonstrated that the *Corpus Hermeticum* was a forgery.[10] Those who

---

[10] Umberto Eco, *Foucault's Pendulum* translated by William Weaver (London, 1989).

have followed my first two lectures know it, and if they read *Foucault's Pendulum* they can find some analogy between what the great philologist understood and what my character finally understands. I was aware that few readers would have been able to catch the allusion, but I was equally aware that, in terms of textual strategy, this was not indispensable (I mean that one can read my novel and understand my Casaubon even though disregarding the historical Casaubon – many authors like to put in their texts certain shibboleths for a few smart readers). Before finishing my novel I discovered by chance that Casaubon was also a character of *Middlemarch*, a book that I had read decades ago and which does not rank among my *livres de chevet*. That was a case in which, as a Model Author, I made an effort to eliminate a possible reference to George Eliot. At page 63 of the English translation can be read the following exchange between Belbo and Casaubon:

'By the way, what's your name?'
'Casaubon.'
'Casaubon. Wasn't he a character in *Middlemarch*?'
'I don't know. There was also a Renaissance philologist by that name, but we are not related.'

I did my best to avoid what I thought to be a useless reference to Mary Ann Evans. But then came a smart reader, David Robey, who remarked that, evidently not by chance, Eliot's Casaubon was writing *A Key to All Mythologies*. As a Model Reader I feel obliged to accept that innuendo. Text plus standard encyclopedia knowledge entitle any cultivated reader to find that connection. It makes sense. Too bad for the empirical author who was not as smart as his reader. In the same vein, my last novel is entitled *Foucault's Pendulum* because the pendulum I am speaking of was invented by Léon Foucault. If it were invented by Franklin the title would have been *Franklin's Pendulum*. This time I was aware from the very beginning that somebody could have smelled an allusion to Michel Foucault: my characters are obsessed by analogies and Foucault wrote on the paradigm of similarity. As an empirical author I was not so happy about such a possible connection. It sounds like a joke and not a clever one, indeed. But the pendulum invented by Léon was the hero of my story and I could not change the title: thus I hoped that my Model Reader would not try to make a superficial connection with Michel. I was to be disappointed; many smart readers did so. The text is there, and maybe they are right: maybe I am responsible for a superficial joke; maybe the joke is not that superficial. I do not know. The whole affair is by now out of my control.

Giosue Musca wrote a critical analysis of my last novel that I consider among the best I have read.[11] From the beginning, however, he confesses to having been corrupted by the habit of my characters and goes fishing for analogies. He masterfully isolates many ultraviolet quotations and stylistic analogies I wanted to be discovered; he finds other connections I did not think of but that look very persuasive; and he plays the role of a paranoiac reader by finding out connections that amaze me but that I am unable to disprove – even though I know that they can mislead the reader. For instance, it seems that the name of the computer, Abulafia, plus the names of the three main characters – Belbo, Casaubon, and Diotallevi – produces the series ABCD. Useless to say that until the end of my work I gave the computer a different name: my readers can object that I unconsciously changed it just in order to obtain an alphabetic series. It seems that Jacopo Belbo is fond of whisky and his initials make 'J and B'. Useless to say that until the end of my work his first name was Stefano and that I changed it into Jacopo at the last moment.

---

[11] Giosue Musca, 'La camicia del nesso', *Quaderni Medievali*, 27 (1989).

The only objections I can make as a Model Reader of my book are (a) the alphabetical series ABCD is textually irrelevant if the names of the other characters do not bring it to X, Y, and Z; and (b) Belbo also drinks Martinis and his mild alcoholic addiction is not the most relevant of his features. On the contrary I cannot disprove my reader's remark that Pavese was born in a village called Santo Stefano Belbo and that my Belbo, a melancholic Piedmontese, can recall Pavese. It is true that I spent my youth on the banks of the river Belbo (where I underwent some of the ordeals that I attributed to Jacopo Belbo, and a long time before I was informed of the existence of Cesare Pavese). But I knew that by choosing the name Belbo my text would have in some way evoked Pavese. And it is true that by designing my Piedmontese character I also thought of Pavese. Thus my Model Reader is entitled to find such a connection. I can only confess (as an empirical author, and as I said before) that in a first version the name of my character was *Stefano* Belbo. Then I changed it into Jacopo, because – as a model author – I did not want my text to make such a blatantly perceptible connection. Evidently this was not enough, but my readers are right. Probably they would be right even if I called Belbo by any other name.

I could keep going with examples of this sort, and I have chosen only those that were more immediately comprehensible. I skipped other more complex cases because I risked engaging myself too much in matters of philosophical or aesthetical interpretation. I hope my listeners will agree that I have introduced the empirical author in this game only in order to stress his irrelevance and to reassert the rights of the text.

As I draw to the end of my lectures, however, I have the sense that I have scarcely been generous to the empirical author. Still, there is at least one case in which the witness of the empirical author acquires an important function. Not so much in order to understand his texts better, but certainly in order to understand the creative process. To understand the creative process is also to understand how certain textual solutions come into being by serendipity, or as the result of unconscious mechanisms. It is important to understand the difference between the textual strategy – as a linguistic object that the Model Readers have under their eyes (so that they can go on independently of the empirical author's intentions) – and the story of the growth of that textual strategy.

Some of the examples I have given can work in this direction. Let me add now two other curious examples which have a certain privileged status: they really concern only my personal life and do not have any detectable textual counterpart. They have nothing to do with the business of interpretation. They can only tell how a text, which is a machine conceived in order to elicit interpretations, sometimes grows out of a magmatic territory which has nothing – or not yet – to do with literature.

First Story. In *Foucault's Pendulum* the young Casaubon is in love with a Brazilian girl called Amparo. Giosue Musca found, tongue-in-cheek, a connection with André Ampère, who studied the magnetic force between two currents. Too smart. I did not know why I chose that name: I realized that it was not a Brazilian name, so I was compelled to write, 'I never did understand how it was that Amparo, a descendant of Dutch settlers in Recife who intermarried with Indians and Sudanese blacks – with her Jamaican face and Parisian culture – had wound up with a Spanish name.'[12] This means that I took the name Amparo as if it came from outside my novel. Months after the publication of the novel a friend asked me: 'Why Amparo? Is it not the name of a mountain?' And then he explained,

---

[12] *Foucault's Pendulum*, p. 161.

'There is that song, "Guajira Guantanamera", which mentions a mount Amparo.'

Oh my God. I knew that song very well, even though I did not remember a single word of it. It was sung, in the mid-fifties, by a girl with whom I was in love. She was Latin American, and very beautiful. She was not Brazilian, not Marxist, not black, not hysterical, as Amparo is, but it is clear that, when inventing a Latin American charming girl, I unconsciously thought of that other image of my youth, when I was the same age as Casaubon. I thought of that song, and in some way the name Amparo (that I had completely forgotten) transmigrated from my unconscious to the page. This story is entirely irrelevant for the interpretation of my text. As far as the text is concerned Amparo is Amparo is Amparo is Amparo.

Second Story. Those who have read my *Name of the Rose* know that there is a mysterious manuscript, that it contains the lost second book of Aristotle's *Poetics*, that its pages are anointed with poison and that it is described like this:

He read the first page aloud, then stopped, as if he were not interested in knowing more, and rapidly leafed through the following pages. But after a few pages he encountered resistance, because near the upper corner of the side edge, and along the top, some pages had stuck together, as happens when the damp and deteriorating papery substance forms a kind of sticky paste.[13]

I wrote these lines at the end of 1979. In the following years, perhaps also because after *The Name of the Rose* I started to be more frequently in touch with librarians and book collectors (and certainly because I had a little more money at my disposal) I became a regular collector of rare books. It has happened

---

[13] Umberto Eco, *The Name of the Rose*, translated by William Weaver (New York: Harcourt Brace, 1983; pb. ed., New York, Warner Books, 1984), p. 570. British edition by Secker & Warburg.

before, in the course of my life, that I bought some old book, but by chance, and only when it was very cheap. Only in the last decade have I become a serious book collector, and 'serious' means that one has to consult specialized catalogues and must write, for every book, a technical file, with the collation, historical information on the previous or following editions, and a precise description of the physical state of the copy. This last job requires technical jargon in order to be precise: foxed, browned, water-stained, soiled, washed or crisp leaves, cropped margins, erasures, re-baked bindings, rubbed joints, and so on.

One day, rummaging through the upper shelves of my home library I discovered an edition of the *Poetics* of Aristotle with comments by Antonio Riccoboni, Padua, 1587. I had forgotten I had it: I found on the endpaper '1000' written in pencil, which meant that I had bought it somewhere for 1,000 lires (less than fifty pence), probably twenty or more years before. My catalogues said that it was the second edition, not exceedingly rare, and that there was a copy of it at the British Museum; but I was happy to have it because it was somewhat difficult to find and in any case the commentary of Riccoboni is less known and less quoted than those, let's say, of Robertello or Castelvetro.

Then I started writing my description. I copied the title page and I discovered that the edition had an Appendix; 'Ejusdem Ars Comica ex Aristotele'. This meant that Riccoboni had tried to reconstruct the lost second book of the *Poetics*. It was not, however, an unusual endeavour, and I went on to set up the physical description of the copy. Then, what had happened to a certain Zatesky, as described by Lurija,[14] happened to me: having lost part of his brain during the war, and with that part

---

[14] A.R. Lurija, *Man with a Shattered World* (New York, Basic, 1972).

of the brain the whole of his memory and of his speaking ability, Zatesky was nevertheless still able to write: thus automatically his hand wrote down all the information he was unable to think of, and step by step he reconstructed his own identity by reading what he was writing. Likewise, I was looking coldly and technically at the book, writing my description, and suddenly I realized that I was rewriting the *Name of the Rose*. The only difference was that from page 120, when the 'Ars Comica' begins, the lower and not the upper margins were severely damaged; but all the rest was the same, the pages progressively browned and stained from dampness and at the end stuck together, looking as if they were smeared by a disgusting fat substance. I had in my hands, in printed form, the manuscript I described in my novel. I had had it for years and years within reach, at home.

At first I thought it was an extraordinary coincidence; then I was tempted to believe in a miracle; at the end I decided that *wo Es war, soll Ich werden*. I had bought that book in my youth, skimmed through it, realized that it was exceptionally soiled, and put it somewhere and forgot it. But by a sort of internal camera I had photographed those pages, and for decades the image of those poisonous leaves lay in the most remote part of my soul, as in a grave, until the moment it emerged again (I do not know for what reason) and I believed I had invented it.

This story, too, has nothing to do with a possible interpretation of my book. If it has a moral it is that the private life of the empirical authors is in a certain respect more unfathomable than their texts. Between the mysterious history of a textual production and the uncontrollable drift of its future readings, the text qua text still represents a comfortable presence, the point to which we can stick.

4

The pragmatist's progress

RICHARD RORTY

When I read Professor Eco's novel *Foucault's Pendulum*, I decided that Eco must be satirizing the way in which scientists, scholars, critics and philosophers think of themselves as cracking codes, peeling away accidents to reveal essence, stripping away veils of appearance to reveal reality. I read the novel as anti-essentialist polemic, as a spoof of the metaphor of depth – of the notion that there are deep meanings hidden from the vulgar, meanings which only those lucky enough to have cracked a very difficult code can know. I took it as pointing up the similarities between Robert Fludd and Aristotle – or, more generally, between the books you find in the 'Occult' sections of bookstores and the ones you find in the 'Philosophy' sections.

More specifically, I interpreted the novel as a send-up of structuralism – of the very idea of structures which stand to texts or cultures as skeletons to bodies, programs to computers, or keys to locks. Having previously read Eco's *A Theory of Semiotics* – a book which sometimes reads like an attempt to crack the code of codes, to reveal the universal structure of structures – I concluded that *Foucault's Pendulum* stood to that earlier book as Wittgenstein's *Philosophical Investigations* to his *Tractatus Logico-Philosophicus*. I decided that Eco had managed to shrug off the diagrams and taxonomies of his earlier work, just as the older Wittgenstein shrugged off his youthful fantasies of ineffable objects and rigid connections.

I found my interpretation confirmed in the last fifty pages of the novel. At the beginning of those pages we find ourselves caught up in what purports to be an axial moment of history. This is the moment in which the hero, Casaubon, sees all the earth's seekers after the One True Meaning of Things assembled at what they believe to be the World's Navel. The Cabbalists, the Templars, the Masons, the Pyramidologists, the Rosicrucians, the Voodooists, the emissaries from the Central Ohio Temple of the Black Pentacle – they are all there, whirling around Foucault's pendulum, a pendulum which is now weighted with the corpse of Casaubon's friend Belbo.

From this climax the novel slowly spirals down to a scene of Casaubon alone in a pastoral landscape, an Italian hillside. He is in a mood of wry abjuration, relishing small sensory pleasures, cherishing images of his infant child. A few paragraphs from the very end of the book, Casaubon meditates as follows:

Along the Bricco's slopes are rows and rows of vines. I know them, I have seen similar rows in my day. No doctrine of numbers can say if they are in ascending or descending order. In the midst of the rows – but you have to walk barefoot, with your heels callused, from childhood – there are peach trees ... When you eat the peach, the velvet of the skin makes shudders run from your tongue to your groin. Dinosaurs once grazed there. Then another surface covered theirs. And yet, like Belbo when he played the trumpet, when I bit into the peach I understood the Kingdom and was one with it. The rest is only cleverness. Invent; invent the Plan, Casaubon. That's what everyone has done, to explain the dinosaurs and the peaches.

I read this passage as describing a moment like that when Prospero breaks his staff, or when Faust listens to Ariel and abandons the quest of Part I for the ironies of Part II. It reminded me of the moment when Wittgenstein realized that the important thing is to be able to stop doing philosophy when one wants to, and of the moment when Heidegger concluded that he must overcome all overcoming and leave metaphysics to itself. By reading the passage in terms of these parallels, I was able to call up a vision of the great magus of Bologna renouncing structuralism and abjuring taxonomy. Eco, I decided, is telling us that he is now able to enjoy dinosaurs, peaches, babies, symbols and metaphors without needing to cut into their smooth flanks in search of hidden armatures. He is willing at last to abandon his long search for the Plan, for the code of codes.

By interpreting *Foucault's Pendulum* in this way I was doing the same sort of thing as is done by all those monomaniacal sectarian taxonomists who whirl round the pendulum. These people eagerly fit anything that comes along into the secret history of the Templars, or the ladder of Masonic enlightenment, or the plan of the Great Pyramid, or whatever their particular obsession happens to be. Shudders run from their cerebral cortices to their groins as they share the delights which Paracelsus and Fludd knew – as they discover the true significance of the fuzziness of peaches, seeing this microcosmic fact as corresponding to some macrocosmic principle. Such people take exquisite pleasure in finding that their key has opened yet another lock, that still another coded message has yielded to their insinuations and given up its secrets.

My own equivalent of the secret history of the Templars – the grid which I impose on any book I come across – is a semi-autobiographical narrative of the Pragmatist's Progress. At the beginning of this particular quest romance, it dawns on the Seeker after Enlightenment that all the great dualisms of Western Philosophy – reality and appearance, pure radiance and diffuse reflection, mind and body, intellectual rigour and sensual sloppiness, orderly semiotics and rambling semiosis –

can be dispensed with. They are not to be synthesized into higher unities, not *aufgehoben*, but rather actively forgotten. An early stage of Enlightenment comes when one reads Nietzsche and begins thinking of all these dualisms as just so many metaphors for the contrast between an imagined state of total power, mastery and control and one's own present impotence. A further state is reached when, upon rereading *Thus Spake Zarathustra*, one comes down with the giggles. At that point, with a bit of help from Freud, one begins to hear talk about the Will to Power as just a high-faluting euphemism for the male's hope of bullying the females into submission, or the child's hope of getting back at Mummy and Daddy.

The final stage of the Pragmatist's Progress comes when one begins to see one's previous peripeties not as stages in the ascent toward Enlightenment, but simply as the contingent results of encounters with various books which happened to fall into one's hands. This stage is pretty hard to reach, for one is always being distracted by daydreams: daydreams in which the heroic pragmatist plays a Walter Mitty-like role in the immanent teleology of world history. But if the pragmatist can escape from such daydreams, he or she will eventually come to think of himself or herself as, like everything else, capable of as many descriptions as there are purposes to be served. There are as many descriptions as there are uses to which the pragmatist might be put, by his or her self or by others. This is the stage in which all descriptions (including one's self-description as a pragmatist) are evaluated according to their efficacy as instruments for purposes, rather than by their fidelity to the object described.

So much for the Pragmatist's Progress – a narrative I often use for purposes of self-dramatization, and one into which I was charmed to find myself being able to fit Professor Eco. Doing so enabled me to see both of us as having overcome our earlier ambitions to be code-crackers. This ambition led me to waste my twenty-seventh and twenty-eighth years trying to discover the secret of Charles Sanders Peirce's esoteric doctrine of 'the reality of Thirdness' and thus of his fantastically elaborate semiotico-metaphysical 'System'. I imagined that a similar urge must have led the young Eco to the study of that infuriating philosopher, and that a similar reaction must have enabled him to see Peirce as just one more whacked-out triadomaniac. In short, by using this narrative as a grid, I was able to think of Eco as a fellow-pragmatist.

This agreeable sense of camaraderie began to evaporate, however, when I read Eco's article 'Intentio lectoris'.[1] For in that article, written at roughly the same time as *Foucault's Pendulum*, he insists upon a distinction between *interpreting* texts and *using* texts. This, of course, is a distinction we pragmatists do not wish to make. On our view, all anybody ever does with anything is use it.[2] Interpreting something, knowing it, penetrating to its essence, and so on are all just various ways of describing some process of putting it to work. So I was abashed to realize that Eco would probably view my reading of his novel as a use rather than an interpretation, and that he did not think much of non-interpretative uses of texts. I was dismayed to find him insisting on a distinction similar to E.D. Hirsch's distinction between meaning and significance – a distinction between getting inside the text itself and relating the text to something else. This is exactly the sort of distinction anti-essentialists like me deplore – a distinction between inside

[1] The texts of Eco's actual Tanner lectures were not available to the seminarists in advance, but he had suggested that we consult his article 'Intentio lectoris: the state of the art', *Differentia*, 2 (1988), 147–68.

[2] For a nice succinct statement of this pragmatist view of interpretation, see Jeffrey Stout, 'What is the meaning of a text?', *New Literary History*, 14 (1982), 1–12.

" and outside, between the non-relational and the relational
" features of something. For, on our view, there is no such thing
" as an intrinsic, non-relational property.

In these comments, therefore, I am going to focus on Eco's
use–interpretation distinction, doing my best to minimize its
importance. I begin with one of Eco's own polemical applic-
ations of this distinction – his account, in 'Intentio lectoris', of
how Marie Bonaparte spoiled her own treatment of Poe. Eco
says that when Bonaparte detected 'the same underlying
fabula' in 'Morella', 'Ligeia' and 'Eleonora', she was 'revealing
the *intentio operis*'. But, he continues, 'Unfortunately, such a
beautiful textual analysis is interwoven with biographical
remarks that connect textual evidence with aspects (known by
extratextual sources) of Poe's private life.' When Bonaparte
invokes the biographical fact that Poe was morbidly attracted
by women with funereal features, then, Eco says, 'she is using
and not interpreting texts'.

My first attempt to blur this distinction consists in noting
that the boundary between one text and another is not so clear.
Eco seems to think that it was all right for Bonaparte to read
'Morella' in the light of 'Ligeia'. But why? Merely because of
the fact that they were written by the same man? Is that not
being unfaithful to 'Morella', and running the danger of
confusing the *intentio operis* with an *intentio auctoris* inferred
from Poe's habit of writing a certain sort of text? Is it fair for me
to read *Foucault's Pendulum* in the light of *A Theory of Semiotics*
and *Semantics and the Philosophy of Language*? Or should I, if I
want to interpret the first of these books, try to bracket my
knowledge that it was written by the author of the other two?

If it is all right for me to invoke this knowledge about
authorship, how about the next step? Is it all right for me to
bring in my knowledge of what it is like to study Peirce – of
what it is like to watch the hearty pragmatist of the 1870s

transmogrify into the frenzied constructor of Existential Graphs of the 1890s? Can I fairly use my biographical knowledge of Eco, my knowledge that he spent a lot of time on Peirce, to help explain his having written a novel about occultist monomania?

These rhetorical questions are the initial softening-up moves I would make in order to begin to blur Eco's use–interpretation distinction. But the big push comes when I ask why he *wants* to make a great big distinction between the text and the reader, between *intentio operis* and *intentio lectoris*. What purpose is served by doing so? Presumably Eco's answer is that it helps you respect the distinction between what he calls 'internal textual coherence' and what he calls 'the uncontrollable drives of the reader'. He says that the latter 'controls' the former, and that the only way to check a conjecture against the *intentio operis* 'is to check it against the text as a coherent whole'. So presumably we erect the distinction as a barrier to our monomaniacal desire to subdue everything to our own needs.

One of those needs, however, is to convince other people that we are right. So we pragmatists can view the imperative to check your interpretation against the text as a coherent whole simply as a reminder that, if you want to make your interpretation of a book sound plausible, you cannot just gloss one or two lines or scenes. You have to say something about what most of the *other* lines or scenes are doing there. If I wanted to persuade you to accept my interpretation of *Foucault's Pendulum*, I should have to account for the thirty-nine pages which intervene between the climactic *Walpurgisnacht* scene in Paris and the peaches and dinosaurs of Italy. I should have to offer a detailed account of the role of the recurrent flashbacks to partisan activities during the Nazi occupation. I should have to explain why, after the moment of abjuration, the last paragraphs of the book introduce a threatening note. For Casaubon ends his pastoral idyll by forseeing his imminent death at the hands of the pursuing monomaniacs.

I do not know whether I could do all this. It is possible that, given three months of leisure and a modest foundation grant, I might produce a graph which connected all or most of these and other dots, a graph which still profiled Eco as a fellow-pragmatist. It is also possible that I would fail, and would have to admit that Eco had other fish than mine to fry, that my own monomania was not flexible enough to accommodate his interests. Whatever the outcome, I agree with Eco that such a graph would be needed before you could decide whether my interpretation of *Foucault's Pendulum* was worth taking seriously.

But given this distinction between a first blush, brute force, unconvincing application of a particular reader's obsession to a text and the product of a three-months-long attempt to make that application subtle and convincing, do we need to describe it in terms of the notion 'the text's intention'? Eco makes clear that he is not claiming that that intention can narrow interpretations down to a single correct one. He happily admits that we can 'show how Joyce [in *Ulysses*] acted in order to create many alternative figures in the carpet, without deciding how many they can be and which of them are the best ones'. So he thinks of the intention of the text rather as the production of a Model Reader, including 'a Model Reader entitled to try infinite conjectures'.

What I do not understand in Eco's account is his view of the relation between those latter conjectures and the intention of the text. If the text of *Ulysses* has succeeded in getting me to evisage a plurality of figures to be found in the carpet, has its internal coherence done all the controlling it can do? Or can it also control the responses of those who wonder whether some given figure is really in the carpet or not? Can it help them choose between competing suggestions – help separate the best interpretation from its competitors? Are its powers exhausted after it has rejected those competitors which are simply unable to connect enough dots – unable to answer enough questions about the function of various lines and scenes? Or does the text have powers in reserve which enable it to say things like 'that graph does, indeed, connect most of my points, but it nevertheless gets me all wrong'?

My disinclination to admit that any text can say such a thing is reinforced by the following passage in Eco's article. He says 'the text is an object that the interpretation builds up in the course of the circular effort of validating itself on the basis of what it makes up as its result'. We pragmatists relish this way of blurring the distinction between finding an object and making it. We like Eco's redescription of what he calls 'the old and still valid hermeneutic circle'. But, given this picture of texts being made as they are interpreted, I do not see any way to preserve the metaphor of a text's *internal* coherence. I should think that a text just has whatever coherence it happened to acquire during the last roll of the hermeneutic wheel, just as a lump of clay only has whatever coherence it happened to pick up at the last turn of the potter's wheel.

So I should prefer to say that the coherence of the text is not something it has before it is described, any more than the dots had coherence before we connected them. Its coherence is no more than the fact that somebody has found something interesting to say about a group of marks or noises – some way of describing those marks and noises which relates them to some of the other things we are interested in talking about. (For example, we may describe a given set of marks as words of the English language, as very hard to read, as a Joyce manuscript, as worth a million dollars, as an early version of *Ulysses*, and so on). This coherence is neither internal nor external to anything; it is just a function of what has been said so far about those marks. As we move from relatively uncontroversial philology and book chat into relatively controversial literary history and literary criticism, what we say must have some reasonably systematic inferential connections with what we or others have previously said – with previous descriptions of these same marks. But there is no point at which we can draw a line between what we are talking about and what we are saying about it, except by reference to some particular purpose, some particular *intentio* which *we* happen, at the moment, to have.

These, then, are the considerations I should bring to bear against Eco's use–interpretation distinction. Let me now turn to a more general difficulty I have with his work. When I read Eco or any other writer on language, I naturally do so in the light of my own favourite philosophy of language – Donald Davidson's radically naturalistic and holistic view. So my first question, on reading Eco's 1984 book, *Semiotics and the Philosophy of Language* (immediately after reading *Foucault's Pendulum*) was: how close is Eco going to come to Davidsonian truth?

Davidson follows through on Quine's denial of an interesting philosophical distinction between language and fact, between signs and non-signs. I hoped that my interpretation of *Foucault's Pendulum* – my reading of it as what Daniel Dennett calls 'a cure for the common code' – might be confirmed, despite the disconfirmation I had found in 'Intentio lectoris'. For I hoped that Eco would show himself at least somewhat less attached to the notion of 'code' than he had been when, in the early 1970s, he wrote *A Theory of Semiotics*. My hopes were raised by some passages in *Semiotics and the Philosophy of Language* and cast down by others. On the one hand, Eco's suggestion that we think about semiotics in terms of labyrinthine inferential relations

within an encyclopedia, rather than in terms of dictionary-like
relations of equivalence between sign and thing signified,
seemed to me to be pointing in the right holistic, Davidsonian,
direction. So did his Quinean remarks that a dictionary is just
a disguised encyclopedia, and that 'any encyclopedia-like
semantics must blur the distinction between analytic and
synthetic properties'.[3]

On the other hand, I was troubled by Eco's quasi-Diltheyan
insistence on distinguishing the 'semiotic' from the 'scientific',
and on distinguishing philosophy from science[4] – an un-
Quinean, un-Davidsonian thing to do. Further, Eco always
seemed to be taking for granted that signs and texts were quite
different from other objects – objects such as rocks and trees
and quarks. At one point he writes:

The universe of semiosis, that is, the universe of human culture, must
be conceived as structured like a labyrinth of the third type: (a) it is
structured according to a *network of interpretants*. (b) It is virtually
infinite because it takes into account multiple interpretations realized
by different cultures ... it is infinite because every discourse about
the encyclopedia casts in doubt the previous structure of the
encyclopedia itself. (c) It does not register only 'truths' but, rather,
what has been said about the truth or what has been believed to be
true ...[5]

This description of 'the universe of semiosis ... the universe of
human culture' seems to be a good description of the universe
tout court. As I see it, the rocks and the quarks are just more
grist for the hermeneutic process of making objects by talking
about them. Granted, one of the things we say when we talk
about rocks and quarks is that they antedate us, but we often
say that about marks on paper as well. So 'making' is not the

[3] Umberto Eco, *Semiotics and the Philosophy of Language* (Bloomington, Ind.,
1986), p. 73.   [4] See ibid., p. 10.   [5] Ibid., pp. 83–4.

right word either for rocks or for marks, any more than is 'finding'. We don't exactly make them, nor do we exactly find them. What we do is to react to stimuli by emitting sentences containing marks and noises such as 'rock', 'quark', 'mark', 'noise', 'sentence', 'text', 'metaphor' and so on.

We then infer other sentences from these, and others from those, and so on – building up a potentially infinite labyrinthine encyclopedia of assertions. These assertions are always at the mercy of being changed by fresh stimuli, but they are never capable of being *checked against* those stimuli, much less against the internal coherence of something outside the encyclopedia. The encyclopedia can get *changed* by things outside itself, but it can only be *checked* by having bits of itself compared with other bits. You cannot *check* a sentence against an object, although an object can *cause* you to stop asserting a sentence. You can only check a sentence against other sentences, sentences to which it is connected by various labyrinthine inferential relationships.

This refusal to draw a philosophically interesting line between nature and culture, language and fact, the universe of semiosis and some other universe, is where you wind up when, with Dewey and Davidson, you stop thinking of knowledge as accurate representation, of getting the signs lined up in the right relations to the non-signs. For you also stop thinking that you can separate the object from what you say about it, the signified from the sign, or the language from the metalanguage, except ad hoc, in aid of some particular purpose. What Eco says about the hermeneutic circle encourages me to think that he might be more sympathetic to this claim than his essentialist-sounding distinction between interpretation and use would at first suggest. These passages encourage me to think that Eco might someday be willing to join Stanley Fish and Jeffrey Stout in offering a *thoroughly* pragmatic account of interpretation, one which no longer contrasts interpretation with use.

Another aspect of Eco's thought which encourages me to think this is what he says about deconstructive literary criticism. For, many of the things which Eco says about this kind of criticism parallel what we Davidsonians and Fishians say about it. In the final paragraphs of 'Intentio lectoris' Eco says that 'many of the examples of deconstruction provided by Derrida' are 'pretextual readings, performed not in order to interpret the text but to show how much language can produce unlimited semiosis'. I think this is right, and that Eco is also right when he goes on to say:

> It so happened that a legitimate philosophical practice has been taken as a model for literary criticism and for a new trend in textual interpretation ... It is our theoretical duty to acknowledge that this happened and to show why it should not have happened.[6]

Any explanation of why this unfortunate thing happened would bring us back, sooner or later, to the work and influence of Paul de Man. I agree with Professor Kermode that Derrida and de Man are the two men who 'give genuine prestige to theory'. But I think it important to emphasize that there is a crucial difference between the two men's theoretical outlooks. Derrida, on my reading, never takes philosophy as seriously as de Man does, nor does he wish to divide language, as de Man did, into the kind called 'literary' and some other kind. In particular, Derrida never takes the metaphysical distinction between what Eco calls 'the universe of semiosis' and some other universe – between culture and nature – as seriously as de Man did. De Man makes heavy use of the standard Diltheyan distinction between 'intentional objects' and

6 Eco, 'Intentio lectoris', 166.

'natural objects'. He insists on contrasting language and its imminent threat of incoherence, produced by 'universal semiosis', with the putatively coherent and unthreatened rocks and quarks.[7] Derrida, like Davison, edges away from these distinctions, viewing them as just more remnants of the Western metaphysical tradition. De Man, on the other hand, makes them basic to his account of reading.

We pragmatists wish that de Man had not sounded this Diltheyan note, and that he had not suggested that there is an area of culture called 'philosophy' which can lay down guidelines for literary interpretation. More particularly, we wish he had not encouraged the idea that you could, by following these guidelines, find out what a text is 'really about'. We wish that he had dropped the idea that there is a special kind of language called 'literary language' which reveals what language itself 'really is'. For the prevalence of such ideas seems to me largely responsible for the unfortunate idea that reading Derrida on metaphysics will give you what Eco calls 'a model for literary criticism'. De Man offered aid and comfort to the unfortunate idea that there is something useful called the 'deconstructive method'.

For us pragmatists, the notion that there is something a given text is *really* about, something which rigorous application of a method will reveal, is as bad as the Aristotelian idea that there is something which a substance really, intrinsically, *is* as opposed to what it only apparently or accidentally or relationally is. The thought that a commentator has discovered what a

7 See Paul de Man, *Blindness and Insight*, (Minneapolis, 2nd ed., 1983), p. 24 for de Man's straightforwardly Husserlian way of distinguishing between 'natural objects' and 'intentional objects'. This is an opposition which Derrida would hardly wish to leave unquestioned. See also de Man, *The Resistance to Theory* (Minneapolis, 1986), p. 11, where de Man opposes 'language' to 'the Phenomenal world,' as well as *Blindness*, p. 110, where he opposes 'scientific' texts to 'critical' texts.

text is really doing – for example, that it is *really* demystifying an ideological construct, or *really* deconstructing the hierarchical oppositions of western metaphysics, rather than merely being capable of being *used* for these purposes – is, for us pragmatists, just more occultism. It is one more claim to have cracked the code, and thereby detected What Is *Really* Going On – one more instance of what I read Eco as satirizing in *Foucault's Pendulum*.

But opposition to the idea that texts are really about something in particular is also opposition to the idea that one particular interpretation might, presumably because of its respect for 'the internal coherence of the text', hit upon what that something is. More generally, it is opposition to the idea that the text can tell you something about what *it* wants, rather than simply providing stimuli which make it relatively hard or relatively easy to convince yourself or others of what you were initially inclined to say about it. So I am distressed to find Eco quoting Hillis Miller with approval when Miller says: 'the readings of deconstructive criticism are not the wilful imposition by a subjectivity of a theory on the texts, but are coerced by the texts themselves'.[8] To my ear, this is like saying that my use of a screwdriver to drive screws is 'coerced by the screwdriver itself' whereas my use of it to pry open cardboard packages is 'wilful imposition by subjectivity'. A deconstructor like Miller, I should have thought, is no more entitled to invoke this subjectivity–objectivity distinction than are pragmatists like Fish, Stout and myself. People who take the hermeneutic circle as seriously as Eco does should, it seems to me, also eschew it.

To enlarge on this point, let me drop the screwdriver and use a better example. The trouble with screwdrivers as an example

---

8 J. Hillis Miller, 'Theory and practice', *Critical Inquiry* 6 (1980), 611, quoted in Eco, 'Intentio lectoris', 163.

is that nobody talks about 'finding out how they work', whereas both Eco and Miller talk this way about texts. So let me instead use the example of a computer program. If I use a particular word-processing program for writing essays, nobody will say that I am wilfully imposing my subjectivity. But the outraged author of that program might conceivably say this if she finds me using it to make out my income tax return, a purpose for which that particular program was never intended and for which it is ill-suited. The author might want to back her point up by enlarging on how her program works, going into detail about the various subroutines which make it up, their marvellous internal coherence and their utter unsuitability for purposes of tabulation and calculation. Still, it would be odd of the programmer to do this. To get her point, I do not need to know about the cleverness with which she designed the various subroutines, much less about how they look in BASIC or in some other compiler language. All she really needs to do is to point out that I can get the sort of tabulations and computations I need for the tax return out of her program only through an extraordinarily inelegant and tedious set of manoeuvres, manoeuvres I could avoid if I were only willing to use the right tool for the right purpose.

This example helps me to make the same criticism of Eco on the one hand and of Miller and de Man on the other. For the moral of the example is that you should not seek more precision or generality than you need for the particular purpose at hand. I see the idea that you can learn about 'how the text works' by using semiotics to analyse its operation as like spelling out certain word-processing subroutines in BASIC: you can do it if you want to, but it is not clear why, for most of the purposes which motivate literary critics, you should bother. I see the idea that what de Man calls 'literary language' has as its function the dissolution of the traditional metaphysical oppositions, and that *reading* as such has something to do with hastening this dissolution, as analogous to the claim that a quantum-mechanical description of what goes on inside your computer will help you understand the nature of programs in general.

In other words, I distrust both the structuralist idea that knowing more about 'textual mechanisms' is essential for literary criticism and the post-structuralist idea that detecting the presence, or the subversion, of metaphysical hierarchies is essential. Knowing about mechanisms of textual production or about metaphysics can, to be sure, sometimes be useful. Having read Eco, or having read Derrida, will often give you something interesting to say about a text which you could not otherwise have said. But it brings you no closer to what is *really* going on in the text than having read Marx, Freud, Matthew Arnold or F.R. Leavis. Each of these supplementary readings simply gives you one more context in which you can place the text – one more grid you can place on top of it or one more paradigm to which to juxtapose it. Neither piece of knowledge tells you anything about the nature of texts or the nature of reading. For neither has a nature.

Reading texts is a matter of reading them in the light of other texts, people, obsessions, bits of information, or what have you, and then seeing what happens. What happens may be something too weird and idiosyncratic to bother with – as is probably the case with my reading of *Foucault's Pendulum*. Or it may be exciting and convincing, as when Derrida juxtaposes Freud and Heidegger, or when Kermode juxtaposes Empson and Heidegger. It may be *so* exciting and convincing that one has the illusion that one now sees what a certain text is *really* about. But what excites and convinces is a function of the needs and purposes of those who are being excited and convinced. So it seems to me simpler to scrap the distinction between using and interpreting, and just distinguish between uses by different people for different purposes.

I think that resistance to this suggestion (which was made most persuasively, I think, by Fish) has two sources. One is the philosophical tradition, going back to Aristotle, which says that there is a big difference between practical deliberation about what to do and attempts to discover the *truth*. This tradition is invoked when Bernard Williams says, in criticism of Davidson and me: 'There is clearly such a thing as practical reasoning or deliberation, which is not the same as thinking about how things are. It is *obviously* not the same . . .'[9] The second source is the set of intuitions which Kant marshalled when he distinguished between value and dignity. Things, Kant said, have value, but persons have dignity. Texts are, for this purpose, honorary persons. To merely use them – to treat them merely as means and not also as ends in themselves – is to act immorally. I have inveighed elsewhere against the Aristotelian practice–theory and the Kantian prudence–morality distinctions, and I shall try not to repeat myself here. Instead, I want briefly to say what can be salvaged from both distinctions. For there is, I think, a useful distinction which is vaguely shadowed forth by these two useless distinctions. This is between knowing what you want to get out of a person or thing or text in advance and hoping that the person or thing or text will help you want something different – that he or she or it will help you to change your purposes, and thus to change your life. This distinction, I think, helps us highlight the difference between methodical and inspired readings of texts.

Methodical readings are typically produced by those who lack what Kermode, following Valéry, calls 'an appetite for

<hr/>

[9] Bernard Williams, *Ethics and the Limits of Philosophy* (Cambridge, MA, 1985), p. 135.

poetry'.[10] They are the sort of thing you get, for example, in an anthology of readings on Conrad's *Heart of Darkness* which I recently slogged through – one psychoanalytic reading, one reader-response reading, one feminist reading, one deconstructionist reading, and one new historicist reading. None of the readers had, as far as I could see, been enraptured or destabilized by *Heart of Darkness*. I got no sense that the book had made a big difference to them, that they cared much about Kurtz or Marlow or the woman 'with helmeted head and tawny cheeks' whom Marlow sees on the bank of the river. These people, and that book, had no more changed these readers' purposes than the specimen under the microscope changes the purpose of the histologist.

Unmethodical criticism of the sort which one occasionally wants to call 'inspired' is the result of an encounter with an author, character, plot, stanza, line or archaic torso which has made a difference to the critic's conception of who she is, what she is good for, what she wants to do with herself: an encounter which has rearranged her priorities and purposes. Such criticism uses the author or text not as a specimen reiterating a type but as an occasion for changing a previously accepted taxonomy, or for putting a new twist on a previously told story. Its respect for the author or the text is not a matter of respect for an *intentio* or for an internal structure. Indeed, 'respect' is the wrong word. 'Love' or 'hate' would be better. For a great love or a great loathing is the sort of thing that changes us by changing our purposes, changing the uses to which we shall put people and things and texts we encounter later. Love and loathing are both quite different from the jovial camaraderie which I imagined myself sharing with Eco when I

---

10 See Frank Kermode, *An Appetite for Poetry* (Cambridge, MA, 1989), pp. 26–7.

treated *Foucault's Pendulum* as grist for my pragmatic mill – as a splendid specimen of a recognizable, greetable, type.

It may seem that in saying all this I am taking the side of so-called 'traditional humanistic criticism' against the genre for which, as Professor Culler has said, the most convenient designation is the nickname 'theory'.[11] Although I think that this sort of criticism has been treated rather too harshly lately, this is not my intention. For in the first place, a lot of humanistic criticism was essentialist – it believed that there were deep permanent things embedded in human nature for literature to dig up and exhibit to us. This is not the sort of belief we pragmatists wish to encourage. In the second place, the genre we call 'theory' has done the English-speaking world a lot of good by providing an occasion for us to read a lot of first-rate books we might otherwise have missed – books by Heidegger and Derrida, for example. What 'theory' has not done, I think, is to provide a method for reading, or what Hillis Miller calls 'an ethic of reading'. We pragmatists think that nobody will ever succeed in doing either. We betray what Heidegger and Derrida were trying to tell us when we try to do either. We start succumbing to the old occultist urge to crack codes, to distinguish between reality and appearance, to make an invidious distinction between getting it right and making it useful.

---

[11] See Jonathan Culler, *Framing the Sign: Criticism and its Institutions* (Norman, Okla., 1988), p. 15.

5

In defence of overinterpretation

JONATHAN CULLER

Richard Rorty's essay in this volume is less a response to Umberto Eco's lectures than a comment on an earlier paper of Eco's entitled 'Intentio operis', which developed a somewhat different argument from that pursued in the lectures. I propose to comment on Umberto Eco's lectures, 'Interpretation and overinterpretation', but then will return to some of the points Professor Rorty has raised in his commentary. The pragmatist's conviction that all the old problems and distinctions can be swept away, installing us in a happy monism, where, as Rorty puts it, 'all anybody ever does with anything is to use it', has the virtue of simplicity but the difficulty of neglecting the sorts of problems that Umberto Eco and many others have wrestled with, including the question of how a text can challenge the conceptual framework with which one attempts to interpret it. These are problems which, I think, will not disappear with the pragmatist's injunction not to worry, but simply to enjoy interpretation. But I shall return to these issues later.

When I was invited to take part in this event and told that the title of the series of lectures was 'Interpretation and overinterpretation', I somehow sensed what my role was supposed to be: to defend overinterpretation. Since I had heard Umberto Eco lecture many times, and well knew the wit and exuberant narrative skill he could bring to the mockery of whatever he chose to call overinterpretation, I could see that defending overinterpretation might well prove uncomfortable, but in fact I am happy to accept my allotted role, to defend overinterpretation on principle.

Interpretation itself needs no defence; it is with us always, but like most intellectual activities, interpretation is interesting only when it is extreme. Moderate interpretation, which articulates a consensus, though it may have value in some circumstances, is of little interest. A good statement of this view comes from G.K. Chesterton, who observes, 'Either criticism is no good at all (a thoroughly defensible proposition) or else criticism means saying about an author those very things that would have made him jump out of his boots.'

As I shall stress later, I think that the production of interpretations of literary works should not be thought of as the supreme goal, much less the only goal of literary studies, but if critics are going to spend their time working out and proposing interpretations, then they should apply as much interpretive pressure as they can, should carry their thinking as far as it can go. Many 'extreme' interpretations, like many moderate interpretations, will no doubt have little impact, because they are judged unpersuasive or redundant or irrelevant or boring, but if they are extreme, they have a better chance, it seems to me, of bringing to light connections or implications not previously noticed or reflected on than if they strive to remain 'sound' or moderate.

Let me add here that, whatever Umberto Eco may say, what he does in these three lectures, as well as what he has written in his novels and his works of semiotic theory, convinces me that deep down, in his hermetical soul which draws him to those whom he calls the 'followers of the veil', he too believes that overinterpretation is more interesting and intellectually valuable than 'sound', moderate interpretation. No one who was not deeply attracted to 'overinterpretation' could create the characters and the interpretive obsessions that animate his novels. He spends no time in the lectures collected here telling us what a sound, proper, moderate interpretation of Dante would say but a good deal of time reviving, breathing life into an outrageous nineteenth-century Rosicrucian interpretation of Dante – an interpretation which, as he said, had had no impact on literary criticism and had been completely ignored until Eco uncovered it and set his students to work on this interesting semiotic practice.

But if we are to make any progress in thinking about interpretation and overinterpretation, we must pause to consider the opposition itself, which is somewhat tendentious. The idea of 'overinterpretation' not only begs the question of which is to be preferred, but it also, I believe, fails to capture the problems Professor Eco himself wishes to address. One might imagine *overinterpretation* to be like *overeating*: there is proper eating or interpreting, but some people don't stop when they should. They go on eating or interpreting in excess, with bad results. Consider, though, the two principal cases Umberto Eco gives us in his second lecture. Rossetti's writing on Dante didn't produce a normal, proper interpretation and then go too far, interpret too much, or interpret excessively. On the contrary, as I understand it, at least, what vitiates Rossetti's interpretation of Dante are two problems, the combination of which is lethal and ensured his neglect until Professor Eco revived him. First, he attempted to draw a Rosicrucian thematics from elements of a motif which in fact do not appear together in Dante and some of which – for instance, the Pelican – appear rarely anywhere in the poem, so that this argument is not persuasive. Second, he sought to explain the importance of these motifs (which he had failed to demonstrate) as the influence of a supposedly prior tradition, for which no independent evidence exists. The problem here is scarcely overinterpretation, if anything it is underinterpretation: a failure to interpret enough elements of the poem, and failure to look at actual prior texts to find in them concealed Rosicrucianism and determine possible relations of influence.

The second example Professor Eco offers in his second lecture is a perfectly harmless piece of belletristic interpretation of Wordsworth's 'A slumber did my spirit seal' by Geoffrey Hartman. Hartman, who is linked to deconstruction by metonymy – by his contiguity at Yale to people such as Paul de Man, Barbara Johnson, J. Hillis Miller and Jacques Derrida, who were engaged in deconstructive reading – is in this example displaying in a rather traditional way what has been known as literary sensibility or sensitivity: hearing in a verse echoes of other verses, words, or images. For instance, in 'diurnal' – a latinate word which does indeed stand out in the context of the simple diction of Wordsworth's poem – he hears suggestions of a funeral motif, a potential pun: '*die-urn*-al'. And he hears the word *tears* 'potentially evoked', as he puts it, by the rhyming series of *fears*, *hears*, *years*. This mild, modest interpretive passage might *become* something like overinterpretation if Hartman were to make strong claims – arguing for instance that 'trees' does not *belong* in the last line of the poem ('Rolled round in earth's diurnal course, / With rocks and stones and *trees*') because trees do not roll as rocks and stones and tears do. Further, he might have argued, the more natural order of an earlier line ('She neither hears nor sees') would have been 'She neither sees nor hears', which would have demanded as the concluding rhyme word something like *tears*, instead of *trees*. Therefore he might have concluded, like a good 'follower of the veil', the secret meaning of this little poem is really the repression of *tears*, for which *trees* has been substituted (you can't see the wood for the trees). That might have been overinterpretation, but it also might have been more interesting and illuminating of the poem (even if we were finally to reject it) than what Hartman actually wrote, which seems, as I say, an admirable traditional exercise of literary sensibility to identify 'suggestions' lurking in and behind the language of the poem.

A clearer instance of overinterpretation might be, as in Eco's example of interpretations of *believe me*, the reflection on the significance of set or idiomatic phrases that have a regular social meaning. If I greet an acquaintance by saying as we pass on the sidewalk, 'Hullo, lovely day, isn't it?', – I don't expect him to walk on muttering something like, 'I wonder what on earth he meant by that? Is he so committed to undecidability that he can't tell whether it is a lovely day or not and has to seek confirmation from me? Then why didn't he wait for an answer, or does he think *I* can't tell what sort of day it is that he has to tell me? Is he suggesting that *today*, when he passed me without stopping, is a lovely day by contrast with yesterday, when we had a long conversation?' This is what Eco calls *paranoid interpretation*, and if our interest is in simply receiving messages that are sent, then paranoid interpretation may be counterproductive, but at least in any academic world, with things the way they are, I suspect that a little paranoia is essential to the just appreciation of things.

Moreover, if our interest is not so much in the receiving of intended messages but in understanding, say, the mechanisms of linguistic and social interaction, then it is useful from time to time to stand back and ask why someone said some perfectly straightforward thing such as, 'Lovely day, isn't it?' What does it mean that *this* should be a casual form of greeting? What does that tell us about this culture as opposed to others that might have different phatic forms or habits? What Eco calls *overinterpretation* may in fact be a practice of asking precisely those questions which are *not* necessary for normal communication but which enable us to reflect on its functioning.

In fact, I think this problem in general and the problems Eco wants to address are better captured by an opposition Wayne Booth formulated a few years ago in a book called *Critical Understanding*: instead of *interpretation* and *overinterpretation*, he contrasted *understanding* and *overstanding*. *Understanding* he conceived as Eco does, in terms of something like Eco's model reader. Understanding is asking the questions and finding the answers that the text insists on. 'Once upon a time there were three little pigs' demands that we ask 'So what happened?' and not 'Why three?' or 'What is the concrete historical context?', for instance. *Overstanding*, by contrast, consists of pursuing questions that the text does not pose to its model reader. One advantage of Booth's opposition over Eco's is that it makes it easier to see the role and importance of overstanding than when this sort of practice is tendentiously called overinterpretation.

As Booth recognizes, it can be very important and productive to ask questions the text does *not* encourage one to ask about it. To illustrate the pursuit of overstanding he asks,

What do you have to say, you seemingly innocent child's tale of three little pigs and a wicked wolf, about the culture that preserves and responds to you? About the unconscious dreams of the author or folk that created you? About the history of narrative suspense? About the relations of the lighter and the darker races? About big people and little people, hairy and bald, lean and fat? About triadic patterns in human history? About the Trinity? About laziness and industry, family structure, domestic architecture, dietary practice, standards of justice and revenge? About the history of manipulations of narrative point of view for the creation of sympathy? Is it good for a child to read you or hear you recited, night after night? Will stories like you – *should* stories like you – be allowed when we have produced our ideal socialist state? What are the sexual implications of that chimney – or of this strictly male world in which sex is never mentioned? What about all that huffing and puffing?[1]

All this overstanding would count as overinterpretation, I think. If interpretation is reconstruction of the intention of the text, then these are questions that don't lead that way; they ask about what the text does and how: how it relates to other texts and to other practices; what it conceals or represses; what it advances or is complicitous with. Many of the most interesting forms of modern criticism ask not what the work has in mind but what it forgets, not what it says but what it takes for granted.

To take the elucidation of the text's intention as the goal of literary studies is what Northrop Frye in his *Anatomy of Criticism* called the Little Jack Horner view of criticism: the idea that the literary work is like a pie into which the author 'has diligently stuffed a specific number of beauties or effects' and that the critic, like Little Jack Horner, complacently pulls them out one by one, saying, 'O what a good boy am I.' Frye called this idea, in a rare fit of petulance, 'One of the many slovenly illiteracies that the absence of systematic criticism has allowed to grow up.'[2]

The alternative for Frye, of course, is a poetics which attempts to describe the conventions and strategies by which literary works achieve the effects they do. Many works of literary criticism are interpretations in that they talk about particular works, but their aim may be less to reconstruct the meaning of those works than to explore the mechanisms or structures by which they function and thus to illuminate

---

[1] Wayne Booth, *Literary Understanding: The Power and Limits of Pluralism* (Chicago, University of Chicago Press, 1979), p. 243.

[2] Northrop Frye, *Anatomy of Criticism: Four Essays* (Princeton, Princeton University Press, 1957), p. 17.

general problems about literature, narrative, figurative language, theme, and so on. Just as linguistics does not seek to
interpret the sentences of a language but to reconstruct the
system of rules that constitutes it and enables it to function, so
a good deal of what may be mistakenly seen as overinterpretation or somewhat better, as overstanding, is an attempt to
relate a text to the general mechanisms of narrative, of
figuration, of ideology, and so on. And semiotics, the science of
signs, of which Umberto Eco is the most distinguished
representative, is precisely the attempt to identify the codes
and mechanisms through which meaning is produced in
various regions of social life.

The decisive issue in Professor Rorty's response to Eco is not
therefore his claim that there is no difference between using a
text (for our own purposes) and interpreting it – that both of
these are just uses of the text – but rather his claim that we
should abandon our search for codes, our attempt to identify
structural mechanisms, and simply enjoy 'dinosaurs, peaches,
babies and metaphors' without cutting into them and trying to
analyse them. At the end of his response he comes back to this
claim, arguing that there is no need for us to bother trying to
find out how texts work – this would be like spelling out word-
processing subroutines in BASIC. We should just use texts as we
use word-processors, in an attempt to say something
interesting.

But in this claim we do find a distinction between using a
word-processing program and analysing it, understanding it,
perhaps improving it or adapting it to purposes it serves only
clumsily. Rorty's own appeal to this distinction might be taken
to refute his claim that all anyone ever does with a text is to use
it, or at least to indicate that there are significant differences
among ways of using a text. In fact, we could follow up on
Rorty's point by arguing that, while for many significant

purposes, it is not important to find out how computer programs or natural languages or literary discourses work, for the academic study of these subjects – computer science, linguistics, and literary criticism and theory – the point is precisely to attempt to understand how these languages work, what enables them to function as they do, and under what circumstances they might function differently. The fact that people can speak English perfectly well without worrying about its structure does not mean that the attempt to describe its structure is pointless, only that the goal of linguistics is not to make people speak English better.

What is confusing in literary studies is that many people are in fact attempting to analyse aspects of the language, the system, the subroutines of literature if you will, while presenting what they are doing as an interpretation of the literary works. It may therefore seem that, as Rorty might put it, they are just using literary works to tell stories about the myriad problems of human existence. Such uses of literary works may, on occasion, involve little concern with or investigation of how these works function, but most of the time such concern and such investigation is in fact crucial to the project, even if it is not stressed in the interpretive narrative. But the point is that the attempt to understand how literature works is a valid intellectual pursuit, though not of interest to everyone, like the attempt to understand the structure of natural languages or the properties of computer programs. And the idea of literary study as a discipline is precisely the attempt to develop a systematic understanding of the semiotic mechanisms of literature, the various strategies of its forms.

What is missing from Rorty's response, therefore, is any sense that literary studies might consist of more than loving and responding to characters and themes in literary works. He can imagine people using literature to learn about themselves –

certainly a major use of literature – but not, it seems, learning something about literature. It is surprising that a philosophical movement that styles itself 'Pragmatism' should neglect this eminently practical activity of learning more about the functioning of important human creations, such as literature; for whatever epistemological problems might be posed by the idea of 'knowledge' of literature, it is clear that practically, in studying literature, people do not just develop interpretations (uses) of particular works but also acquire a general understanding of how literature operates – its range of possibilities and characteristic structures.

But more than this neglect of institutional realities of knowledge, what I have always found particularly disquieting about contemporary American Pragmatism – of Rorty and Fish, for example – is that people who attained their positions of professional eminence by engaging in spirited debate with other members of an academic field, such as philosophy or literary studies, by identifying the difficulties and inconsistencies of their elders' conceptions of the field and by proposing alternative procedures and goals, have, once they attain professional eminence, suddenly turned and rejected the idea of a system of procedures and body of knowledge where argument is possible and presented the field as simply a group of people reading books and trying to say interesting things about them. They thus seek systematically to destroy the structure through which they attained their positions and which would enable others to challenge them in their turn. Stanley Fish, for instance, established himself by offering theoretical arguments about the nature of literary meaning and the role of the reading process and claiming that his predecessors who had pronounced on this topic were wrong. Once he had reached a position of eminence, however, he turned around and said, 'Actually, there isn't anything here one could be right or wrong about; there isn't such a thing as the nature of literature or of reading; there are only groups of readers and critics with certain beliefs who do whatever it is that they do. And there is no way in which other readers can challenge what I do because there is no position outside belief from which the validity of a set of beliefs could be adjudicated.' This is a less happy version of what Rorty, in his response, calls 'Pragmatist's progress'.

Richard Rorty's own *Philosophy and the Mirror of Nature* is a powerful work of philosophical analysis precisely because it grasps the philosophical enterprise as a system with a structure and shows the contradictory relations between various parts of that structure – relations which put in question the foundational character of that enterprise. To tell people they should give up attempting to identify underlying structures and systems but just use texts for their own purposes is to attempt to block other people from doing work like that for which he gained recognition. Similarly, it is all very well to say that students of literature should not bother trying to understand how literature works but should just enjoy it or read on in the hope of finding a book that will change their life. Such a vision of literary study, though, by denying any public structure of argument in which the young or marginalized could challenge the views of those who currently occupy positions of authority in literary studies, helps make those positions unassailable and in effect confirms a structure in place by denying that there is a structure.

Thus it seems to me that the crucial issue in Rorty's reply is not a question of the distinction (or lack of distinction) between interpretation and use but the claim that we should not bother to understand how texts work any more than we should seek to understand how computers work because we can use them perfectly well without much knowledge. Literary studies, I insist, is precisely the attempt to gain such knowledge.

I want to comment on a curious point of convergence yet disagreement in Professor Eco's and Rorty's discussions. One thing they share is a desire to dismiss deconstruction, which shared desire suggests that, contrary to popular report, deconstruction must be alive and well. Curiously, however, Eco and Rorty give very nearly opposing descriptions of deconstruction. Umberto Eco seems to take it as the extreme form of reader-oriented criticism, as if it said that a text means anything a reader wants it to mean. Richard Rorty, on the other hand, faults deconstruction and Paul de Man in particular, for refusing to give up the idea that structures are truly *in* the text and that they force themselves on the reader, whose deconstructive reading only identifies what is already there in the text. Rorty faults deconstruction for maintaining that there are basic textual structures or mechanisms and that one can find out things about how a text works. Deconstruction, in his view, is wrong because of its failure to accept that readers just have different ways of using texts, none of which tell you something 'more basic' about the text.

In this disagreement – does deconstruction say that a text means what a reader wants it to mean or does it say that it has structures that have to be discovered? – Rorty is more nearly right than Eco. His account, at least, helps to explain how deconstruction could claim that a text might undermine categories or disrupt expectations. I believe that Eco has been misled by his concern with limits or boundaries. He wants to say that texts give a great deal of scope to readers but that there are limits. Deconstruction, on the contrary, stresses that meaning is context bound – a function of relations within or between texts – but that context itself is boundless: there will always be new contextual possibilities that can be adduced, so that the one thing we *cannot* do is to set limits. Wittgenstein asks, 'Can I say "Bububu" and mean, if it does not rain I shall go out for a walk?' And he replies, 'it is only in a language that one can mean something by something'.[3] This may appear to establish limits, maintaining that 'Bububu' could never mean this, unless the language were different, but the way in which language works, especially literary language, prevents this establishment of a limit or firm boundary. Once Wittgenstein produced this positing of a limit it became possible in certain contexts (especially in the presence of those who know Wittgenstein's writings) to say 'Bububu' and at least allude to the possibility that if it does not rain one might go for a walk. But this lack of limits to semiosis does not mean, as Eco seems to fear, that meaning is the free creation of the reader. It shows, rather, that describable semiotic mechanisms function in recursive ways, the limits of which cannot be identified in advance.

In his critique of deconstruction for its failure to become a happy pragmatics, Rorty suggests that de Man believes philosophy provides guidelines for literary interpretation. This is a misconception that should be corrected: de Man's engagement with philosophical texts is always critical and, in a sense, literary — attuned to their rhetorical strategies; he scarcely draws from them anything like a *method* for literary interpretation. But it is certainly true that he does not believe that philosophy and philosophical questions can be left behind, as Rorty seems to. Deconstructive readings characteristically show how the problems posed by traditional philosophical distinctions prove ubiquitous, turn up repeatedly,

---

[3] Ludwig Wittgenstein, *Philosophical Investigations* (Oxford, Blackwell, 1963), p. 18.

even in the most 'literary' of works. It is this continuing engagement with the hierarchical oppositions which structure Western thought, and the recognition that the belief one has overcome them once and for all is likely to be a facile delusion, that give deconstruction a critical edge, a critical role. These hierarchical oppositions structure concepts of identity and the fabric of social and political life, and to believe one has gone beyond them is to risk complacently abandoning the enterprise of critique, including the critique of ideology.

Roland Barthes, who was congenitally given to hesitating between poetics and interpretation, once wrote that those who do not re-read condemn themselves to read the same story everywhere.[4] They recognize what they already think or know. Barthes' claim was, in effect, that some sort of method for 'overinterpretation' – for instance, an arbitrary procedure that divided the text up into sequences and required that each be examined closely and its effects spelled out, even if it did not seem to pose interpretive problems – was a way to make discoveries: discoveries about the text and about the codes and practices that enable one to play the role of reader. A method that compels people to puzzle over not just those elements which might seem to resist the totalization of meaning but also those about which there might initially seem to be nothing to say has a better chance of producing discoveries – though like everything else in life there is no guarantee here – than one which seeks only to answer those questions that a text asks its model reader.

At the beginning of his second lecture Umberto Eco linked overinterpretation to what he called an 'excess of wonder', an excessive propensity to treat as significant elements which might be simply fortuitous. This *déformation professionelle*, as

4 Roland Barthes, *S/Z* (Paris, Seuil, 1970), pp. 22–3.

he sees it, which inclines critics to puzzle over elements in a text, seems to me, on the contrary, the best source of the insights into language and literature that we seek, a quality to be cultivated rather than shunned. It would be sad indeed if fear of 'overinterpretation' should lead us to avoid or repress the state of wonder at the play of texts and interpretation, which seems to me all too rare today, though admirably represented in the novels and semiotic explorations of Umberto Eco.

6

Palimpsest history[1]

CHRISTINE BROOKE-ROSE

My title is adapted from a notion, by now familiar but particularly well-expressed in Salman Rushdie's novel *Shame*. The notion is that of history as itself a fiction, the expression is varied. First a short quote: 'All stories', he says as intruding author, 'are haunted by the ghosts of the stories they might have been' (116). And now a long quote:

Who commandeered the job of rewriting history? The immigrants, the *mohajris*. In what languages? Urdu and English, both imported tongues. It is possible to see the subsequent history of Pakistan as a duel between two layers of time, the obscured world forcing its way back through what-had-been-imposed. It is the true desire of every artist to impose his or her vision on the world; and Pakistan, the peeling, fragmenting palimpsest, increasingly at war with itself, may be described as a failure of the dreaming mind. Perhaps the pigments used were the wrong ones, impermanent, like Leonardo's; or perhaps the place was just *insufficiently imagined*, a picture full of irreconcilable elements, midriffbaring immigrant saris versus demure, indigenous Sindhi shalwar-kurtas, Urdu versus Punjabi, now versus then: a miracle that went wrong.

As for me: I too, like all migrants, am a fantasist. I build imaginary countries and try to impose them on the ones that exist. I too, face the

---

[1] A version of this paper has also been published as Chapter 12 of *Stories, Theories and Things* (Cambridge University Press, 1991).

problem of history: what to retain, what to dump, how to hold on to what memory insists on relinquishing, how to deal with change.

My story's palimpsest country has, I repeat, no name of its own.[2]

A few lines later, however, he retells the apocryphal story of Napier who, having conquered Sind in what is now South Pakistan, 'sent back to England the guilty, one word message, "Peccavi": *I have Sind*', and adds 'I'm tempted to name my looking-glass Pakistan in honour of this bilingual (and fictional, because never really uttered) pun. Let it be *Peccavistan*.' (88).

And earlier he had said, also as intruding author: 'But suppose this were a realistic novel! Just think what else I might have to put in.' There follows a long paragraph-full of real horrors, with real names, as well as real comic incidents, which ends: 'Imagine my difficulties!' And he goes on:

By now, if I had been writing a book of this nature, it would have done me no good to protest that I was writing universally, not about Pakistan. The book would have been banned, dumped in the rubbish bin, burned. All that effort for nothing. Realism can break a writer's heart.

Fortunately, however, I am only telling a sort of modern fairy-tale, so that's all right; nobody need get upset, or take anything I say too seriously. No drastic action need be taken either.

What a relief!

The semi-conscious dramatic irony of this last passage is poignant.

For of course, all these quotations also apply, in advance of time, to *The Satanic Verses*,[3] where two palimpsest countries, India and England, and one palimpsest religion, Islam, are concerned; and which belongs to a type of fiction that has burst on the literary scene in the last quarter of this century and

---

[2] Salman Rushdie, *Shame* (London, Jonathan Cape, 1985), pp. 87–8.
[3] Rushdie, *The Satanic Verses* (London, Penguin Viking, 1988).

thoroughly renewed the dying art of the novel. *Terra Nostra* by the Mexican Carlos Fuentes,[4] and *Dictionary of the Khazars* by the Yugoslav Milorad Pavić,[5] are other great examples. Some have called this development 'magic realism'. I prefer to call it palimpsest history. It began, I believe, with *A Hundred Years of Solitude* by Gabriel Garcia Márquez,[6] Thomas Pynchon's *Gravity's Rainbow*[7] and Robert Coover's *The Public Burning*.[8] Eco's *The Name of the Rose* and *Foucault's Pendulum* represent another variety. You will note that these are all very big, very long books, and this in itself goes against the trend for novels of some 80,000 words of social comedy or domestic tragedy to which the neorealist tradition had accustomed us for so long. But I'll return to that point later.

First I want to distinguish between various kinds of palimpsest histories:

1 the realistic historical novel, about which I shall say nothing:
2 the totally imagined story, set in a historical period, in which magic unaccountably intervenes (Barth,[9] Márquez):
3 the totally imagined story, set in a historical period, without magic but with so much time-dislocating philosophical, theological and literary allusion and implication that the effect is magical – here I am thinking of Eco; and, in a very different key, partly because the historical period is modern, of Kundera;[10]

4 (London, Secker and Warburg, 1977).
5 (London, Hamilton, 1984).
6 Trans, Gregory Rabassa (New York, Harper and Row, 1967).
7 (New York, Viking, 1973).
8 (New York, Viking, 1977).
9 John Barth, *The Sotweed Factor* (London, Secker and Warburg, 1960).
10 See Milan Kundera *L'Insoutenable légèreté de l'être*, trans. Kerel (1984), revised with author (Paris, Gallimard, 1987); *L'Immortalité*, trans. Eva Bloch and author (Paris, Gallimard, 1990).

4 the zany reconstruction of a more familiar because closer period or event, with apparent magic which is, however, motivated through hallucination, such as the relations between Uncle Sam and Vice-President Nixon in *The Public Burning*, or the great preponderance of paranoiacs in Pynchon's *Gravity's Rainbow*.

Fifthly and lastly, the palimpsest history of a nation and creed, in which magic may or may not be involved but seems almost irrelevant – or shall we say almost natural – compared to the preposterousness of mankind as realistically described. This we find in *Terra Nostra*, *The Satanic Verses*, and *The Dictionary of the Khazars*, which I consider to be far more effective, more significant, and above all more readable and hence truly renewing, than either *The Public Burning* or *Gravity's Rainbow* in my fourth category, with which they seem to have much in common. In fact they are more deeply linked, imaginatively if in different ways, to Márquez, Kundera and Eco, although they look superficially different: Márquez tells an imaginary story of a family travelling and settling, and doesn't bother much with history; while Eco's history, theology, theosophy and so forth are on the face of it scrupulously accurate.

You will have noticed that, if we except Coover and Pynchon, who to my mind do not fully succeed in renewing the novel in this palimpsest way, all the novels discussed are by writers foreign to the Anglo-American novel – for if Rushdie writes in English, and writes very well, renewing the language with Indian words and highly idiomatic expressions, he certainly claims to write as a migrant. The English novel has been dying for a long time, enclosed in its parochial and personal little narrated lives, and if American postmodernism has seemed at times to bring new vigour and a breath of fresh air, it is often still too concerned with the narcissistic relation of the author to his writing, which interests no one but himself. The reader, although frequently addressed, is only taken into account with reference to this narcissistic concern in a 'look-what-I'm-doing' relationship. Here I'm thinking particularly of John Barth, who also writes big novels, or of Gilbert Sorrentino's *Mulligan Stew*.[11] But these have little to do with history, and more to do with either the form of the novel or the modern American Way of Life, or both.

I mentioned Eco's ostensible historical accuracy a moment ago. In contrast, consider the Khazars, a historical but vanished people, mock-reconstructed through biographical entries, in three parts (Christian, Judaic, Islamic), each of which believes the Khazars were converted to its own religion, characters recurring in different versions, with a discreet system of cross-referencing for the reader who wants to read actively rather than passively, and savour the wit.

Or consider Philip II of Spain in *Terra Nostra*. He is shown as a younger man (in his memory), massacring Protestants in Flanders, or later building the Escorial as a permanent mausoleum for his royal ancestors and himself. This is history. But he is also depicted as the son of Felipe el Hermoso (Philip the Handsome), who died young, and Juana la Loca (Joan the Mad), still alive and participating. Now the son of Philip the Handsome and Joan the Mad was the Emperor Charles V. There is a curious fusion of the two. Although often called Felipe, he is mostly referred to as *el Señor*, which could apply to both, and at one point he says 'my name is also Philip' – which makes the reader wonder whether Charles V's second name was Philip. He is also shown as young Philip, forced by his father *el Señor* to take his *droit de cuissage* on a young peasant bride. But later he is said to be married to an English cousin called Isabel,

---

[11]   (London, Marion Boyars, 1980).

which was not true of Philip II, whereas Charles V's queen was called Isabel, but Isabel of Portugal. This English Isabel he never touches, and although he knows she has lovers, he finally separates from her amicably and sends her back to England where she becomes the Virgin Queen Elizabeth. Now, we know that one of Philip's four wives was English, but this was Mary Tudor. Moreover, a constant theme of the novel is that *el Señor* has no heir, and indeed dies heirless, or is at least shown dying in a horrible way and lying still alive in his coffin as he watches the triptych behind the altar, which has curiously changed. Obviously Charles V had an heir, Phillip II, and so did the historical Philip II, by his fourth and Austrian wife, an heir who later became Philip IV. Thus the only historical items are that he besieged a city in Flanders – though Ghent is never named – and that he built the Escorial – that too is never named, only described. And Philip's retreat into this palace of the dead sometimes sounds curiously like Charles's retreat to the monastery at Yurta – which, however he did not build – after his abdication.

A similar fusion or confusion occurs with the New World, to which one of the three triplets and supposed usurpers, who each have six toes and a red cross birthmark on their back, sails on a small boat with one companion, who is killed, and has long and magical adventures in pre-Spanish Mexico. When he returns, Philip refuses to believe in the existence of the Nuevo Mundo which, of course, has historically been well established by his time, since Charles V's empire was one on which, as all the schoolbooks say, the sun never set.

None of this impedes the reading, any more than does the reincarnation of some of the non-royal characters in modern times. Why? Not only because it is a rattling good story in its own right, as convincing as the real story. But also because it is a different view of the human condition and what it endures and springs from, of absolute power and its aberrations, of the way its leaders could discount the deaths of hundreds of workers to build monster palaces, or the deaths of thousands of innocents to build monster dreams, to establish the truth as they saw it. In a way it is what science-fiction theorists call an alternative world.

But science-fiction alternative worlds are either more or less modelled on this one, with some obvious differences required and accepted by the genre; or else they represent our familiar world with some parameter altered, by extraterrestrials or other scientifically impossible event. This is not an alternative world, it is alternative history. Palimpsest history. And there are, incidentally, one or two meditations or fantasies, by Philip especially, of palimpsest religion, that look remarkably heretical or even blasphemous, or at least what Christians would have called heresy or blasphemy in the past. But the Christian authorities have never objected to them. Perhaps they learnt from the Inquisition. Or, more likely, they don't read novels. But then, the condemners of Rushdie, like many of his defenders who speak only on principle and rarely of the book itself, don't seem to have read him either.

Which brings me back to *The Satanic Verses*. Possibly Rushdie had read *Terra Nostra*, since it also contains a character with six toes, though a minor one, and the millions of butterflies that flutter over the pilgrims on their way to the Arabian Sea seem to be inspired by the headdress of live butterflies over the head of the Aztec goddess. But this may be chance. Or allusion. My point is that, whether influenced or not, *The Satanic Verses*, too, is palimpsest history.

Of course we should not be surprised that totalitarian governments, and not least theocratic governments, should, when someone draws their attention to such works, object to palimpsest history. It has happened over and over in the Soviet

Union. Such governments are always busy rewriting history themselves and only *their* palimpsest is regarded as acceptable. And yet there is not a single passage in *The Satanic Verses* that cannot find echo in the Qur'an and qur'anic traditions and Islamic history. The notion of 'Mahound' always receiving messages that justify his double standard with regard to wives, for example, is expressed not by the narrator but by protesting characters in conquered 'Jahilia', and finds its echo in Mohammed's revelations:

Prophet, We have made lawful to you the wives to whom you have granted dowries and the slave-girls whom Allah has given you as booty; the daughters of your paternal and maternal uncles and of your paternal and maternal aunts who fled with you; and the other women who gave themselves to you and whom you wished to take in marriage. This privilege is yours alone, being granted to no other believer.

We well know the duties We have imposed on the faithful concerning their wives and slave-girls. We grant you this privilege so that none may blame you. Allah is forgiving and merciful. (288)

What an easy step in the light-fantastic to imagine that the twelve harlots in the Jahilia brothel should assume the names of the prophet's wives. But Rushdie has explained himself on this. My point is that throughout the book we have a different reading, a poetic, re-creative reading, of what is in the Qur'an. Even the incident of the Satanic Verses finds echo in another context, or rather, in no context at all, when out of the blue Mohammed is told: 'When We change one verse for another (Allah knows best what He reveals), they say: "You are an imposter". Indeed, most of them are ignorant men' (304).

And of course, as Rushdie has insisted, all these re-creative readings are rendered, though less clearly perhaps than univocal readers are used to, as the dreams of Gibreel Farishta, an Indian Muslim actor who often played parts of even Hindu gods in the type of Indian films called 'theologicals'. In other words, the different reading is motivated in much the same way as Pynchon's events are motivated by paranoia. Indeed the use of dreams are part of Rushdie's defence, but personally, and on a purely literary level, I think they are almost a pity, and prefer to read them as fictional facts: why should Gibreel, who falls from the exploded plane and survives, not also travel in time? His companion Saladin after all changes into Shaitan, with growing horns and a tail, and then is suddenly cured. These too are readings, in a way allegorical but also psychological, palimpsest religion. As seen and felt and re-read by a modern sensibility. But as Eco says in 'Intentio lectoris':[12]

Even if one says, as Valéry did, that *il n'y a pas de vrai sens d'un texte*, one has not yet decided on which of the three intentions [planned by the author, ignored by the author, decided by the reader] the infinity of interpretations depends. Medieval and Renaissance Kabbalists maintained that the Torah was open to infinite interpretations because it could be rewritten in infinite ways by combining its letters, but such an infinity of readings (as well as of writings) – certainly dependent on the initiative of the reader – was nonetheless planned by the divine Author.

To privilege the initiative of the reader does not necessarily mean to guarantee the infinity of readings. If one privileges the initiative of the reader, one must also consider the possibility of an active reader who decides to read a text univocally: it is a privilege of fundamentalists to read the Bible according to a single literal sense. (155)

This is certainly what happens with the Qur'an. Only the authorized exegetists are allowed to interpret. A mere author is just nowhere, indeed 'Mahound' is made to say in *The Satanic Verses* that he can see no difference between a poet and a whore. If in addition this author happens to be a non-believer he is even worse than nowhere, for the Qur'an says clearly that Allah chooses the believers and even misleads the unbelievers – a curious concept which reminds us of 'do not lead us into

---

[12] 'Intentio lectoris: the state of the art', *Differentia*, 2 (1988), 147–68.

temptation', though the Pater Noster adds 'but deliver us from evil'. Not so the Qur'an, unless of course the non-believer repents and believes (for Allah is merciful): 'None can guide the people whom Allah leads astray. He leaves them blundering about in their wickedness' (256). As to possible new readings in time, Allah says after a similar passage about unbelievers not being helped: 'Such were the ways of Allah in days gone by: and you shall find that they remain unchanged' (272). Or again: 'Proclaim what is revealed to you in the Book of your Lord. None can change His Words' (92) – except, as we saw, Allah Himself.

Interestingly, the unbelievers are several times shown as accusing Mohammed's revelations of being 'old fictitious tales' (298) or, on the Torah and the Qur'an: '"Two works of magic supporting one another. We will believe in neither of them"' (78). Islam seems to the non-Islamic reader totally anti-narrative. There are no stories in the Qur'an, except one or two brief exempla. This could be regarded as due to the anti-representation rule, if there were not also many bits of stories taken from the Torah (in the wide sense): Tell them about our servant Abraham, Allah says, or Moses, or Lot, or Job, David, Solomon, all the way to Elizabeth and Zachariah or Mary and Jesus. This is admirably syncretic, and the Israelites are called 'the people of the Book'. But the stories themselves are unrecognizable as stories, they are fragmented and repetitive, and occur as 'arguments' and 'signs', and 'proof' of Allah's truth. Apart from these, the Qur'an is amazingly static. There is no narrative line. It is a book of faith and ethics, that establishes a new humanism of a kind, and it proceeds by affirmation and injunction, threats of punishment, examples of destruction, and promises of reward. The story of Mohammed himself comes from other sources. I don't want to venture too far in this, as I am not an Islamist, and no doubt exegesis has different views. No doubt also that other Arabic, and especially Persian, traditions do have stories. My point is simply that from the Qur'an alone, it seems hardly surprising that its more rigid interpreters and followers would be incapable of conceiving, let alone understanding, this new fiction that is palimpsest history, palimpsest religion, or palimpsest history of man's spirituality.

And yet, to a modern sensibility (or at least to mine) – and if it is true, as many sociologists and other observers are saying, that the religious spirit is returning – the agonized doubts of both Gibreel and Saladin, as well as those of Philip II, speak more vividly to us today than can those of the self-centred, sex-centred, whisky-centred, sin-and-salvation-centred characters of Graham Greene, precisely because they are anchored in both ancient and modern history, with its migrations and regenerating mixtures.

I mentioned the sheer size of this type of book, and I would like to end on a more general point, that of knowledge. All the books I have mentioned are large partly because they are packed with specialized knowledge. Pynchon, as Frank Kermode pointed out recently, 'has an enormous amount of expert information – for instance, about technology, history and sexual perversion'.[13] So does Eco about theology and theosophy and literature and philosophy; so does Fuentes about the history of Spain and Mexico; so does Rushdie about Pakistan, India, Hinduism and Islam. Like the historian, these authors work very hard on their facts, So, incidentally, does the author of the more scientific kind of science-fiction.

Now knowledge has long been unfashionable in fiction. If I may make a personal digression here, this is particularly true of women writers, who are assumed to write only of their

13 Frank Kermode, 'Review of Pynchon's *Vineland*', *London Review of Books* (8.2.1990), 3.

personal situations and problems, and I have often been blamed for parading my knowledge, although I have never seen this being regarded as a flaw in male writers; on the contrary. Nevertheless (end of personal digression), even as praise, a show of knowledge is usually regarded as irrelevant: Mr X shows an immense amount of knowledge of a, b, c, and the critic passes to theme, plot, characters and sometimes style, often in that order. What has been valued in this sociological and psychoanalytical century is personal experience and the successful expression of it. In the last resort a novel can be limited to this, can come straight out of heart and head, with at best a craftsmanly ability to organize it well, and write well.

Similarly the Structuralists devoted much analysis to showing how the classical realist novel produced its illusion of reality. Zola did enormous social research on mines and slaughterhouses, and distributed these items of knowledge, as Philippe Hamon has shown,[14] comparing them to index cards, among various pretext-characters to impart, usually to an innocent learner-character, also existing for the purpose. And so on. These various techniques were invented to 'naturalize' culture. But this demystification of the realist illusion does not in fact alter the illusion. 'The nineteenth-century as we know it', said Oscar Wilde, 'is almost entirely an invention of Balzac'. Dickens too had to learn all about law and other spheres of knowledge, Tolstoy all about war, and Thomas Mann a little later all about medicine, music and so on. George Eliot – another knowledgeable novelist, though a woman – said it was not necessary for a writer to experience life in a workshop, the open door was enough. This is obviously true: the writer cannot do without imagination. Dostoevski understood this. And mere homework is not enough either. But a great deal of

---

[14] In Philippe Hamon, 'Un discours contraint', *Poétique* 16 (Paris, Seuil) 411–45; reprinted in *Littérature et réalité* (Paris, Seuil, 1982), pp. 119–81.

this homework done by the classical realist was sociological, and eventually led, in the modern neo-realist novel we are all familiar with, to slice-of-life novels about miners, doctors, football-players, admen and all the rest. Back to the personal experience of the writer in fact. Now personal experience is sadly limited. And the American postmodern attempt to break out of it rarely succeeds beyond fun-games with narrative conventions – a very restricted type of knowledge.

Naturally I am caricaturing a little, to make a point. Naturally I am not trying to say that the polyphonic palimpsest histories I have been discussing are the only great novels of the century, nor that there haven't been other types of highly imaginative novels before these. I am only saying that the novel's task is to do things which only the novel can do, things which the cinema, the theatre and television have to reduce and traduce considerably in adaptations, losing whole dimensions, precisely because they now do better some of what the classical realist novel used to do so well. The novel took its roots in historical documents and has always had an intimate link with history. But the novel's task, unlike that of history, is to stretch our intellectual, spiritual, and imaginative horizons to breaking-point. Because palimpsest histories do precisely that, mingling realism with the supernatural and history with spiritual and philosophical re-interpretation, they could be said to float half-way between the sacred books of our various heritages, which survive on the strength of the faiths they have created (and here I include Homer, who also survived on the absolute faith of the Renaissance in the validity of classical culture), and the endless exegesis and commentaries these sacred books create, which do not usually survive one another, each supplanting its predecessor according to the Zeitgeist, in much the same way as do the translations of Homer or the Russian classics. Pope's Homer is not the Homer of Butcher and

Lang, nor is it as readable today as other poems by Pope. And the Homer of Butcher and Lang isn't anything like Robert Fitzgerald's. It may seem disrespectful to place *The Satanic Verses* half-way between the sacred book that is the Qur'an and the very exegetes who execrate it, but I am here speaking only in literary terms, which may become clearer if I say that Homer is only partially historical, and greatly mythical, or that Fuentes' history of Spain is as interesting as the 'real' history sacralized at school, or Eco's Pendulum as the 'real' history of theosophy. And this is because they are palimpsest histories.

7

Reply

UMBERTO ECO

Richard Rorty's paper represents an outstanding example of close reading of various texts of mine. Yet, if I were convinced by Rorty's reading I should say that it is 'true', thus casting in doubt his liberal attitude towards 'truth'. Probably, to pay homage to such a reader, I should only react in the way he suggested and ask: What was your paper about? However, I admit that my reaction would reproduce the tiresome classical response to the sceptic's argument. And everybody knows that the good sceptic is entitled to react in terms of Orwell's *Animal Farm*: 'OK, all interpreters are equal, but some of them are more equal than others.'

Besides, it would be unjust to ask what Rorty's paper was about. It was undoubtedly about something. It focussed on some alleged contradictions he found between my novel and my scholarly papers. In doing so, Rorty made a strong implicit assumption, namely, that there are family resemblances between different texts by a single author and that all these different texts can be seen as a textual corpus to be investigated in terms of its own coherence. Coleridge would agree, adding that such a tendency to identify the connection of parts to a whole is not a discovery of criticism, but rather a necessity of the human mind – and Culler has shown that such a necessity had also determined the writing of *The Mirror of Nature*.

I understand that, according to a current opinion, I have written some texts that can be labelled as scientific (or academic or theoretical), and some others which can be defined as creative. But I do not believe in such a straightforward distinction. I believe that Aristotle was as creative as Sophocles, and Kant as creative as Goethe. There is not some mysterious ontological difference between these two ways of writing, in spite of many and illustrious 'Defences of Poetry'. The differences stand, first of all, in the propositional attitude of the writers – even though their propositional is usually made evident by textual devices, thus becoming the propositional attitude of the texts themselves.

When I write a theoretical text I try to reach, from a disconnected lump of experiences, a coherent conclusion and I propose this conclusion to my readers. If they do not agree with it, or if I have the impression that they have misinterpreted it, I react by challenging the reader's interpretation. When I write a novel, on the contrary, even though starting (probably) from the same lump of experiences, I realize that I am not trying to impose a conclusion: I stage a play of contradictions. It is not that I do not impose a conclusion because there is no conclusion; on the contrary, there are many possible conclusions (frequently each of them being impersonated by one or more different characters). I refrain from imposing a choice between them not because I do not want to choose but because the task of a creative text is to display the contradictory plurality of its conclusions, setting the readers free to choose – or to decide that there is no possible choice. In this sense a creative text is always an Open Work. The particular role played by language in creative texts – which in some sense are less translatable than the scientific ones – is just due to the necessity to leave the conclusion to float around, to blur the prejudices of the author through the ambiguity of language and the impalpability of a final sense. I challenged Valéry's statement according to which *'il n'y a pas de vrai sens d'un texte'*, but I accept the statement that a text can have many senses. I refuse the statement that a text can have every sense.

There are obviously so-called philosophical texts that belong to the 'creative' category as well as there are so-called 'creative' texts that are didactically imposing a conclusion – where language is unable to realize a situation of openness – but I am designing *Idealtypen*, not classifying concrete texts. Christine Brooke-Rose has spoken of 'palimpsest texts': I think that these texts are simply and more explicitly making their own inner contradiction evident, or that they not only outline a psychological contradictoriness (as happened with old realistic novels), but also a cultural and intellectual one. When they outline the very contradictoriness of the act of writing in itself, they reach a meta-textual status, that is, they speak of their own internal and radical openness.

Rorty's reading of my *Foucault's Pendulum* was very profound and perceptive. He proved to be an Empirical Reader to meet my requirements for the Model Reader I wanted to design. I hope he will not be irritated by my appreciation, but I understand that in saying so I decide that he has not read textuality in general, but he has read *my* novel. The fact that I recognize my novel (and I think that others can do so) through and in spite of his interpretation, does not change my theoretical approach but undoubtedly challenges his own. A text remains as a parameter for his acceptable interpretations.

Now, let me evaluate Rorty's reading not from the point of view of the author (which would be unacceptable from my point of view as a theoretician), but from the point of view of a reader. From such a point of view I believe I am entitled to say that Rorty certainly read *my* novel, but paying attention to some aspects of it and dropping some others. He has used part of my novel for the purposes of his philosophical argument or – as he has suggested – of his own rhetorical strategy. He has only focussed the *pars destruens* of my novel (the against-interpretation-side of it) but he has passed over in silence the textual fact that in my novel, along with the interpretative frenzy of my monomaniacs, there are – I mean, there are as written pages, parts of the same whole – two other examples of interpretation, namely, the interpretation of Lia and the final interpretation of Casaubon who reaches the conclusion that there was an excess of interpretation. It would be embarrassing for me to say that the conclusions of Lia and of Casaubon are offered as if they were *my own* conclusions, and it would be offensive to me to define them as the didactical conclusion of the novel. Notwithstanding this, they are there, as opposed to other possible conclusions.

Rorty can object that he did not detect these other instances of interpretation, and that perhaps the fault is mine. He read in my text what he claimed to have read and nobody can tell that he was simply using my text, otherwise somebody would pretend to have a privileged understanding of my text as an organic whole. Rorty can say that the very fact that he read as he did is an unchallengeable proof that it was possible to read so, and there is no tribunal which can state that his way of reading was less legitimate than mine. At this point – and I apologize if I am overinterpreting Rorty's paper – I ask Rorty why the first page of his paper is so full of *excusationes non petitae* or of prudent apologies of this kind:

'I decided to read . . .'

'I was doing the same sort of things as is done by all those monomaniacal sectarians . . .'

'The grid I impose on any book I come across . . .'

'By using this narrative as a grid, I was able to think of Eco as of a fellow pragmatist . . .'

'Eco would . . . view my reading as a use rather than . . .'

Rorty was evidently aware he was proposing a passional reading of a text which he could have read in other ways (and he seems to know which ones) by respecting other evident aspects of the textual linear manifestation.

I think that we are always reading passionally, by reactions inspired by love or hatred. When, however, we read them twice we discover that – let us say – at the age of twenty we loved a character, and at the age of forty we hate him or her. But usually, if we have literary sensitivity, we realize that that text was so conceived – or happened to look as though it were so conceived – as to elicit both readings. I agree that every property we imputed is non-intrinsic but relational. But if the duty of a scientist is to understand that even gravitation is a three-relational property involving Earth, Sun and a given observer of the Solar system, then even a given interpretation of a text involves: (i) its linear manifestation; (ii) the reader who reads from the point of view of a given *Erwartungshorizon*; and (iii) the cultural encyclopedia comprehending a given language and the series of the previous interpretations of the same text. This third element – about which I shall elaborate in a moment – can only be viewed in terms of responsible and consensual judgement of a community of readers – or of a culture.

To say that there is no *Ding an Sich* and that our knowledge is situational, holistic and constructive, does not mean that when we are speaking we are not speaking of something. To say that this something is relational does not mean that we are not speaking of a *given* relationship. Undoubtedly, the fact that our knowledge is relational and that we cannot separate facts from the language by means of which we express (and construct) them, encourages interpretation. I agree with Culler that even overinterpretation is fruitful, I agree with the idea of hermeneutic suspicion, I am convinced that the fact the Three Little

Pigs are three and not two or four is of some purport. During my lecture, speaking both of interpreters and of other authors and of interpreters of my own novels, I have stressed that it is difficult to say whether an interpretation is a good one, or not. I have however decided that it is possible to establish some limits beyond which it is possible to say that a given interpretation is a bad and far-fetched one. As a criterion, my quasi-Popperian stricture is perhaps too weak, but it is sufficient in order to recognize that *it is not true that everything goes*.

C.S. Peirce, who insisted on the conjectural element of interpretation, on the infinity of semiosis, and on the essential *fallibilism* of every interpretative conclusion, tried to establish a minimal paradigm of acceptability of an interpretation on the grounds of a consensus of the community (which is not so dissimilar from Gadamer's idea of an interpretative tradition). What kind of guarantee can a community provide? I think it provides a factual guarantee. Our species managed to survive by making conjectures that proved to be statistically fruitful. Education consists in telling kids what kind of conjectures proved to be fruitful in the past. *Messer, Feuer, Scherer, Licht – ist für kleine Kinder nicht!* Do not play with fire and knives because it can hurt: it is true because many kids made the opposite conjecture and died.

I think that the cultural community was – if not right, at least reasonable – in telling Leonardo da Vinci it was preposterous to jump from the top of a hill with a pair of flapping wings, because this hypothesis had already been tested by Icarus and proved to be doomed to failure. Perhaps without Leonardo's utopia the posterity would not have been able to keep dreaming of human flight, but human flight became possible only when Leonardo's idea of an aerial screw merged with Huygens' idea of a propeller and with the idea of a rigid wing supported by an aerodynamic force known as 'drag'. That is the reason why the community now recognizes that Leonardo was a great visionary, that is, that he was thinking (unrealistically for his own time, and on the grounds of false assumptions) of future realistic endeavour. But to define him as a utopian genius means exactly that the community recognizes that he was in some way right but in some other way madly wrong.

Rorty suggested that I can use a screwdriver for turning a screw, for opening a package and to scratch my ear inside. This is not a proof that everything goes but rather that objects can be focussed from the point of view of the relevant features – or pertinences – they display. But a screwdriver can also be black, this feature being irrelevant for any purpose (except perhaps if I have to use it to scratch my ear during a formal party in dinner jacket). And I cannot classify a screwdriver among round objects because it does not display the property of being round. We can consider as relevant or pertinent only the features which are detectable by a sane observer – even when they had remained undetected until now – and we can isolate only the features that look perfectly relevant from the point of view of a given purpose.

Frequently we decide to make pertinent certain features that we previously disregarded, in order to use an object for purposes for which it was not explicitly designed. According to an example from Luis Prieto, a metal ashtray was designed as a container (and for this purpose it displays the property of being concave), but since it is also a hard object in some circumstances I can use it as a hammer or as a missile. A screwdriver can be inserted into a cavity and be turned inside, and in this sense could also be used to scratch one's ear. But it is also too sharp and too long to be manoeuvred with millimetric care, and for this reason I usually refrain from introducing it into my ear. A short toothpick with a cotton top will work better. This means that, as well as *impossible pertinences*, there are *crazy pertinences*. I cannot use a screwdriver as an ashtray. I can use a paper glass as an ashtray but not as a screwdriver. I can use a general word-processing software as a stylesheet for my income tax – and as a matter of fact I do use one of the standard packages; but as a result I lose a lot of money, because a spreadsheet designed for such purposes would be more precise.

To decide how a text works means to decide which one of its various aspects is or can become relevant or pertinent for a coherent interpretation of it, and which ones remain marginal and unable to support a coherent reading. The Titanic bumped into an iceberg and Freud lived in Berggasse, but such a pseudo-etymological analogy cannot justify a psychoanalytic explanation of the Titanic case.

Rorty's software example sounds very intriguing. It is true that I can use a particular program without knowing its subroutine. It is also true that a teenager can play with this program and implement functions of which its designer was unaware. But later comes a good computer scientist who dissects the program, looks at its subroutines and not only explains why it was able to perform a given additional function but also reveals why and how it could do many more things. I ask Rorty why the first activity (to use the program without knowing its subroutines) should be considered more respectable than the second one.

I have no objection to people who are using texts for implementing the most daring deconstructions and I confess that frequently I do the same. I like what Peirce called 'the play of musement'. If my purpose were only to live pleasurably, why not use texts as though they were mescalin and why not decide that Beauty is Fun, Fun Beauty, that is all Ye know on Earth, and all ye need to know?

Rorty asked for what purposes we need to know how language works. I respectfully answer: not only because writers study language in order to write better (as far as I remember Culler stressed this point), but also because marvelling (and therefore curiosity) is the source of all knowledge, knowledge is a source of pleasure and it is simply beautiful to discover why and how a given text can produce so many good interpretations.

In my youth I read for the first time *Sylvie* by Gérard de Nerval and I was fascinated by it. During my life I have re-read it many times, and the fascination increased every time. When I read Proust's analysis I realized that the most mysterious feature of *Sylvie* was its ability to create a continuous 'fog effect', an *'effet de brouillard'*, by which we never exactly understand whether Nerval is speaking of the past or of the present, whether the Narrator is speaking about a factual or a remembered experience, and the readers are compelled to turn over the pages backwards to see where they are – their curiosity being always defeated. I tried many times to analyse *Sylvie* to understand by what narrative and verbal strategies Nerval so masterfully succeeded in challenging his reader. I was not satisfied by the pleasure I experienced as an enthralled reader; I also wanted to experience the pleasure of understanding how the text was creating the fog effect I was enjoying.

After many useless efforts, finally I devoted a three-year seminar to this subject, working with a selected bunch of perceptive students, all in love with this novel. The result is now published as *Sur Sylvie*, a special issue of *VS* 31/32, 1982. We hope to have explained – after a quasi-anatomical analysis of every line of that text, scoring the verbal tenses, the different role played by the pronoun *je* as referred to different temporal situations, and so on and so forth – by which semiotic means that text creates its multiple and mutually contradictory effects, and why in the history of its interpretation it was able to elicit and support so many different readings. Due to the fallibilism of knowledge I assume that some further descriptions will discover further semiotic strategies that we have underestimated, just as they may be able to criticize many of our descriptions as effected by an excessive propensity toward hermeneutic suspicion. In any case I presume to have understood better how *Sylvie* works. I also understood why Nerval is not Proust (and vice versa), even though both were obsessively dealing with a *recherche du temps perdu*. Nerval creates the fog effect because, in his quest, he wanted to be and was a loser, while Proust wanted to be and succeeded in being a winner.

Did this kind of theoretical awareness reduce the pleasure and the freedom of my further readings? Not at all. On the contrary, after this analysis I always felt new pleasures and discovered new nuances when re-reading *Sylvie*. To understand how language works does not reduce the pleasure of speaking, and of listening to the eternal murmur of texts. To explain both this feeling and this rational persuasion, I used to say that even gynaecologists fall in love. But if we accept such an obvious remark, we must admit that, whereas we cannot say anything about the feelings of gynaecologists, their knowledge of human anatomy is a matter of cultural consensus.

There is an objection which could be raised about the kind of guarantee provided by the consensus of a community. The objection says that one can accept the control of the community only when one is concerned with the interpretation of stimuli – or of sense data, if such a notion still has an acceptable definition (but in any case I mean to interpret propositions like 'it is raining' or 'salt is soluble'). As Peirce maintained, in interpreting the signs of the world we produce a *habit*, that is, a disposition to act upon reality and to produce other sense data. If I interpret and define, as the alchemists did, certain elements as capable of being transformed into gold, if I elaborate a habit that leads me to try such a transformation, and if at the final end I do not get gold in the crucible, every sane member of the community is entitled to say that my interpretation is – at least up till now – unacceptable because it produced an unsuccessful habit.

By contrast, when dealing with texts, we are not simply dealing with brute stimuli and we are not trying to produce new stimuli: we are dealing with previous interpretations of the world, and the result of our reading (being a new interpretation and not a productive habit) cannot be tested by intersubjective means. But such a distinction seems to me much too rigid. To recognize a sense datum as such we need an interpretation – as well as criterion of pertinence by which certain events are recognized as more relevant than others – and the very result of our operational habits is subject to further interpretation. That is why we believe that the communitarian control of sane partners is enough to decide whether at a given moment it is raining or not, but that the case of the Utah cold fusion looks a little more doubtful. It is however no more or no less doubtful than my previous assertion that there are textual reasons for outlining a difference between Proust and Nerval. In both cases it is a matter of a long series of communitarian controls and revisions.

I know that our certainty that aspirin cures a cold is stronger than our certainty that Proust was aiming at something different from Nerval. There are degrees of acceptability of interpretations. I am more sure that aspirin works to decrease my body temperature than that a given substance can cure cancer. Likewise I am less sure that Proust and Nerval had a different conception of memory than that *Sylvie* was written in a style which is not the style of Proust. And I am pretty sure that Nerval wrote before Proust, even though I cannot rely on personal perceptual experience but I simply trust the community. I know that an atomic bomb was dropped upon Hiroshima in 1945 because I trust the community (though some French scholars declared that the community is unreliable and asserted that the Holocaust was a Jewish invention). Naturally, we have elaborated philological habits by which certain witnesses, certain documents, certain crossed tests must be trusted. Therefore I strongly believe that it is true that Hiroshima was bombed and that Dachau or Buchenwald existed. In the same way I am sure that the Homeric texts, even though of uncertain author, were produced before the *Divine Comedy* and that it is difficult to interpret them as the intended allegory of the Passion of Christ. Naturally I can suggest that the death of Hector is 'a figure of' Christ's Passion, but only after having got the cultural consensus that the Passion is an eternal archetype and not an historical event. The degree of certainty by which I assume that the Narrator of *Sylvie* undergoes experiences that are not those described by the Narrator of Proust is weaker than the degree of certainty by which I assume that Homer wrote before Ezra Pound. But in both cases I rely on the possible consensus of the community.

In spite of the obvious differences in degrees of certainty and uncertainty, every picture of the world (be it a scientific law or a novel) is a book in its own right, open to further interpretation. But certain interpretations can be recognized as unsuccessful because they are like a mule, that is, they are unable to produce new interpretations or cannot be confronted with the traditions of the previous interpretations. The force of the Copernican revolution is not only due to the fact that it explains some astronomical phenomena better than the Ptolemaic tradition, but also to the fact that it — instead of representing Ptolemy as a crazy liar — explains why and on which grounds he was justified in outlining his own interpretation.

I think that we should also deal in this way with literary or philosophical texts and that there are cases in which one has the right to challenge a given interpretation. Otherwise why should I be concerned with the opinions of Richard Rorty, Jonathan Culler or Christine Brooke-Rose? When everybody is right, everybody is wrong and I have the right to disregard everybody's point of view.

Happily I do not think this way. That is the reason for which I thank each of the contributors to this debate, for having provided me with so many challenging insights, and so many interpretations of my work. And I am sure that each of them thinks as I do. Otherwise they would not be here.